U.S. Child Development Laboratory leaders respond to a call to create a research consortium framed by Applied Developmental Science that takes advantage of CDLs' unique histories across nearly 100 years as centers of excellence in early education, professional development, and applied research. Through rich examples from local programs, this volume charts the power and possibility of multi-site efforts to confront many of the large questions and issues facing early childhood education today.

—Mary Jane Moran, Associate Professor, Department of
Child and Family Studies, University of Tennessee

At a time when the relevance and viability of laboratory schools are in question, this volume offers a reconceptualization that enlarges the scope and reach of their work, increases their capacity to impact children, families, practitioners and policy makers, and secures their place on campuses, communities, and the profession.

—Cynthia Paris, Associate Professor, Department of Human Development
and Family Studies, and Director, Early Childhood Laboratory School,
College of Education and Human Development, University of Delaware

D0219808

THE FUTURE OF CHILD DEVELOPMENT LAB SCHOOLS

Child development laboratory schools are found on college and university campuses throughout the U.S. Over the last century, they have acquired a long, rich history. Originally seen as settings for the new field of child study in the early 1900s, their functions have evolved over time. These programs often play a central role in supporting teaching, research, and outreach/engagement activities in the fields of child development and early childhood education. Yet, many have had to fight for their existence when economic times have become difficult. Many long-running programs have had to close.

This book provides a unique perspective on the purpose and function of child development laboratory schools and the potential of large-scale research to examine important world problems. The individual stories presented are real stories that offer reasonable solutions and ideas for maximizing the value of these venerable institutions. Most importantly, the authors demonstrate how child development laboratory schools can address the criticisms often lodged regarding their lack of relevancy and focus on real-life problems and solutions. The range of perspectives includes university faculty trying to maximize research that is applied in nature as well as redefining what and where a laboratory is, both in the university and in the community. The message is clear that child development laboratory schools are alive and well, and continuing to evolve.

Nancy E. Barbour, Ph.D., is a Professor of Early Childhood Education in the College of Education at James Madison University.

Brent A. McBride, Ph.D., is a Professor of Human Development and Director of the Child Development Laboratory at the University of Illinois at Urbana/ Champaign.

THE FUTURE OF CHILD DEVELOPMENT LAB SCHOOLS

Applied Developmental Science in Action

Edited by Nancy E. Barbour and Brent A. McBride

NEW YORK AND LONDON

First published 2017
by Routledge
711 Third Avenue, New York, NY 10017

and by Routledge
2 Park Square, Milton Park, Abingdon, Oxon, OX14 4RN

Routledge is an imprint of the Taylor & Francis Group, an informa business

© 2017 Taylor & Francis

The right of the editors to be identified as the authors of the editorial material, and of the authors for their individual chapters, has been asserted in accordance with sections 77 and 78 of the Copyright, Designs and Patents Act 1988.

Library of Congress Cataloging-in-Publication Data
Names: Barbour, Nancy E., editor. | McBride, Brent A., editor.
Title: The future of child development lab schools: applied developmental science in action / edited by Nancy E. Barbour and Brent A. McBride.
Description: 1st Edition. | New York: Routledge, 2016. | Includes bibliographical references and index.
Identifiers: LCCN 2016020623 | ISBN 9781138898653 (hbk: alk. paper) | ISBN 9781138898660 (pbk: alk. paper) | ISBN 9781315440408 (ebk)
Subjects: LCSH: Laboratory schools—United States. | Early childhood education—United States. | Child development—United States. | Child psychology—United States.
Classification: LCC LB2153.A3 F88 2016 | DDC 370.71/1—dc23
LC record available at https://lccn.loc.gov/2016020623

ISBN: 978-1-138-89865-3 (hbk)
ISBN: 978-1-138-89866-0 (pbk)
ISBN: 978-1-315-44040-8 (ebk)

Typeset in Bembo
by codeMantra

CONTENTS

ABOUT THE EDITORS

Nancy E. Barbour, Ph.D., is a Professor of Early Childhood Education in the College of Education at James Madison University where she teaches and works with accreditation and special projects. She was previously the Associate Dean in the College of Education, Health, and Human Services at Kent State University.

Brent A. McBride, Ph.D., is a Professor of Human Development and Director of the Child Development Laboratory at the University of Illinois at Urbana/Champaign where he works with investigators from a variety of disciplines as they explore protocols and approaches for studying young children's development in the context of classroom environments as well as in laboratory settings.

NOTES ON CONTRIBUTORS

Treshawn Anderson, Ph.D. is an Assistant Professor in Child Development and Family Studies in the Department of Family and Consumer Sciences at California State University, Long Beach. Her research focuses on childcare quality and professional development for practitioners working with children birth to age three.

James Elicker is Professor of Human Development and Family Studies at Purdue University. He is a former Head Start teacher and Director of the university lab school, and currently teaches courses for early childhood education majors. His research focuses on young children's development in the context of early childhood programs.

Diane M. Horm, Ph.D., is the George Kaiser Family Foundation Endowed Chair and Founding Director of the Early Childhood Education Institute at the University of Oklahoma-Tulsa. Diane is currently leading several applied research initiatives focused on children birth through age four.

Jennifer Kampmann serves as the Assistant Department Head in Teaching, Learning, and Leadership at South Dakota State University. Her background is in early childhood education and she is passionate about university outreach with P-12 school partners.

Marjorie Kostelnik is Dean of the College of Education and Human Sciences at the University of Nebraska. She has been associated with Laboratory Schools most of her professional life as a teacher, director, researcher, and academic administrator.

Martha Lash is an Associate Professor of Early Childhood Education and Coordinator of the International Baccalaureate Primary Years Programme Certificate program at

Kent State University. Early childhood education research interests include professional development, curriculum, and international perspectives.

Monica Miller Marsh is Associate Professor and Director of the Kent State University Child Development Center. Her areas of interest include family diversity, early childhood, and curriculum. She is co-founder of the Family Diversity Education Council and the *Journal of Family Diversity in Education*.

Jennifer Ryan Newton is an Assistant Professor of Early Childhood/Early Childhood Special Education in the School of Education at Saint Louis University.

Elizabeth Schlesinger-Devlin, Ed. D. is the Director of the Miller Child Development Laboratory School at Purdue University. Her focus is in fostering research within the context of early childhood programs and applying research findings, particularly in the area of curriculum and instruction, in the early childhood setting.

Andrew J. Stremmel is Professor and Department Head in Teaching, Learning and Leadership at South Dakota State University. His interests are in the area of early childhood teacher education, in particular teacher action research.

Jill Thorngren serves as Dean of the College of Education and Human Sciences at South Dakota State University. Her background is in counseling and she enjoys inter-professional collaborations across several disciplines.

Reece Wilson is an Assistant Professor of Education at James Madison University, where he teaches elementary education courses. He also serves as the Director of JMU's laboratory school, the Young Children's Program.

1

INTRODUCTION

The Future of Child Development Laboratory Schools

Nancy E. Barbour and Brent A. McBride

The following chapters offer a view of the future of child development laboratory settings by applying an Applied Developmental Science (ADS) framework to the work that is done. In doing so, the chapters provide a framework for envisioning the potential power of operating as a collective and collaborative entity. The chapters that follow offer a vision of how child development laboratory settings can maximize their viability on campuses across the country by approaching their roles in a slightly different way.

In our explorations, we are concerned with the long-term viability of child development laboratory settings within the current climate of fiscal scrutiny. How can these venerable, long-running entities become active, vital centers for research that inform service providers, legislators, policymakers, and the public about how best to serve and support young children and families? The chapters provide examples of how faculty at various sites have enacted ADS research, how the status quo on campuses supports or thwarts the potential for ADS research, what possibilities there are for a consortium of laboratory settings to engage in cross-site research, and what a consortium of laboratory settings might be able to accomplish in the world of Applied Developmental Science.

In the early days of the child study movement, Lawrence K. Frank, an economist working for the Laura Spelman Rockefeller Memorial Foundation, had a vision of establishing university sites where research could be done "always with the expectation of science" to solve social problems (Frank, 1962). Since the beginning of child development laboratory settings in the early 20th century, they have at times struggled to achieve this basic element of ADS. However, ADS could be a powerful ally to lab settings in their quest to remain vital in the traditional missions of research, service, and professional preparation. Insights gained from ADS can also inform efforts to reshape activities in lab schools. Finally, the involvement of collaborators from the policy sector may help lab schools truly influence social policy—a long-stated goal that has not been fully realized (McBride et al., 2012). The examination here of how child development labs can collaborate to engage in meaningful, influential, scientific research that has direct implications for individuals in context and can be applied to lifespan developmental issues provides insights for others to explore in their own settings.

As we unpack what ADS is in light of the history of lab schools, we see many connections. Applied Developmental Science is first of all applied work, having direct implications for children, families, policymakers, and practitioners (Lerner, Wertlieb, & Jacobs, 2005). Some of the features of ADS include its **applied** nature: What are the direct implications for children, families, and policymakers? The **developmental** component speaks to the assessment of development across the lifespan and across contexts. **Science** implies the need to consider a variety of methodologies for systematic, intentional inquiry that leads to putting theory into practice (Lerner, Fisher, & Weinberg, 2000). Lerner et al. (2000, p. 14) note the distinction between "efficacy research" that examines what works best "under 'optimal' conditions" and the notion of "outreach" research. ADS research, accordingly, should "engage public policy" and demand collaboration between communities and researchers (Lerner et al., 2000, p. 15). Certainly, the words of Lawrence K. Frank are evoked within these ideals.

Traditionally, child development labs have operated independently, limiting their power to influence policy and practice on a broad scale. What if lab sites joined together to study real-world problems in a variety of community contexts, invoking the essential element of "person-context relations" (Lerner et al., 2005) and employing rigorous research methods to study developmental phenomenon?

Implicit in the process of child development labs engaging in such activity is that they are high quality laboratory settings with "pertinence to human ecology" (Lerner et al., 2005) rather than merely contrived settings. These high quality elements include: a clearly defined mission that connects with the greater good of the community; a mix of both "soft" and "hard" funding sources; collaboration across disciplines, strong personnel, and ongoing professional development; and balance across the three components of lab schools: research, service, and professional preparation (Barbour, 2003). Additionally, a commitment to engage in reciprocal, contextual, and embedded research are important if a child development laboratory consortium is to engage in ADS.

The chapters that follow explore what innovative practices are currently going on in child development laboratories across the country; what possibilities there are for reconceptualizing what constitutes a laboratory; and, finally, an administrator's view of what child development laboratories need to do to survive in the current social, political, and economic climate.

The volume begins with McBride's exploration of a system in place for supporting research and how this system creates a pathway for other programs to maximize research viability and relevance, both in the academy and the "real" world. McBride offers us a vision for what a consortium might be and how a consortium of lab schools might function. The next two chapters examine how two laboratory settings presently engage in research that fits with ADS. In the case of Lash and Miller Marsh's chapter, the authors describe the shift from teacher self-study to different ways of doing research to increase their spheres of influence. In the other example, Schlesinger-Devlin, Elicker, and Anderson share their child development laboratory setting's conceptualization of the different roles that constituents may play in research that fits within the ADS framework.

Stremmel, Kampmann, and Thorngren explore their efforts at expanding their research partners beyond the laboratory and into the community in order to engage in a meaningful and relevant approach to empirical inquiry. They examine both the successes and challenges of doing ADS. Barbour, Wilson, and Ryan Newton offer the case of one program working on the shift from preschool program to laboratory setting, highlighting the many aspects of a high-quality, functional laboratory program. In the penultimate chapter, Horm shares the story of a multi-site collaboration that posits a different way of defining "laboratory." Their research on the Educare program is clearly an example of how research can make an impact on policy. The volume closes with the insightful and provocative musings of Kostelnik as she shares her view from the administrator's seat. She examines what child development laboratories can do in order to thrive, and how their work can raise all boats.

It is our hope that these chapters will provide stimulation for others to think about the potential for child development laboratory settings to be important places of research and innovation. The range of ideas and practices offered here will stimulate new thinking about research that affects the lives of children and families.

References

Barbour, N. E. (2003). The early history of child development laboratory programs. In B. A. McBride & N. E. Barbour (Eds.), *Bridging the gap between theory, research, and practice: The role of child development laboratory programs in early childhood education* (pp. 9–30). New York: Elsevier.

Frank, L. K. (1962). The beginnings of child development and family life education in the twentieth century. *Merrill-Palmer Quarterly of Behavior and Development, 8*(4), 207–227.

Lerner, R. M., Fisher, C. B., & Weinberg, R. A. (2000). Toward a science for and of the people: Promoting civil society through the application of developmental science. *Child Development, 71*, 11–20.

Lerner, R. M., Wertlieb, D., & Jacobs, F. (2005). Historical and theoretical bases of Applied Developmental Science. In R. M. Lerner, F. Jacobs, & D. Wertlieb (Eds.), *Applied Developmental Science: An advanced textbook* (pp. 1–29). Thousand Oaks, CA: Sage.

McBride, B. A., Groves, M., Barbour, N., Horm, D., Stremmel, A., Lash, M., Bersani, C., Ratekin, C., Moran, J., Elicker, J., & Toussaint, S. (2012). Child Development Laboratory schools as generators of knowledge in early childhood education: New models and approaches. *Early Education and Development, 23*(2), 153–164.

2
DATA AND INFRASTRUCTURE SUPPORTS

Critical Components for the Future of Child Development Laboratory Schools

Brent A. McBride

An ever-widening body of knowledge is emerging that identifies a link between quality early childhood program services and children's positive developmental outcomes (Saracho & Spodek, 2012). This literature base suggests that when children attend high quality early childhood programs, positive gains can be seen in such areas as vocabulary development, early math skills, print awareness and pre-reading competencies, and peer relations and social competence. This relationship is especially strong for those children who have been identified as being at-risk for later school failure due to a variety of economic and demographic factors (Pungello et al., 2010).

School readiness has also emerged in recent years as a concern for researchers, educators, and policymakers alike. Research has consistently indicated that the knowledge base and skills that children possess at school entry are highly predictive of their later learning and academic success (Sabol & Pianta, 2012). Thompson (2002) has identified this "readiness" for school as consisting of a combination of young children's intellectual skills, motivational qualities, and socio-emotional skills. Research outlining the benefits of quality early childhood programs would suggest that such initiatives might play a crucial role in helping children to become "ready" for entry into formal schooling. Based on this research, many policymakers have begun to view funding of preschool programs as a mechanism for closing the achievement gap between poor and minority children and their more affluent peers (Hustedt & Barnett, 2011).

In spite of the promise of lasting benefits that can be gained by attending high quality early childhood programs, there is little consensus regarding the exact mechanisms that lead to positive developmental outcomes for children who spend significant amounts of time in group contexts (i.e. child care and preschool classrooms). Much of this research outlining the relationship between program characteristics and children's development draws on data assessing structural (e.g. adult–child ratios, group size) and/or global (e.g. Early Childhood Environmental Rating Scale) indicators of quality as opposed to an examination of those factors that facilitate children's positive growth and development. Such an approach to research in early childhood settings limits our ability to make definitive conclusions about those factors that influence children's learning and development within early childhood classrooms. As a result, policymakers are continually being called upon to make decisions regarding funding of early childhood programs without empirically based insight on the mechanisms underlying children's learning in these settings.

In response to this disconnect between research, policy, and early childhood programming, scholars in the field of early childhood education are beginning to call for a renewed emphasis on research utilizing multi-methods for data collection across diverse disciplines and at different levels of analyses in order to identify and document the mechanisms underlying children's learning. As outlined by others in this edited volume as well as by leading scholars in the field, university-based laboratory schools are uniquely positioned to begin addressing this disconnect (Elicker & Barbour, 2015; McBride et al., 2012).

A new framework for guiding such efforts is needed as laboratory schools explore the possible creation of a consortium that would be better situated to address this disconnect within the early childhood field. The historical perspective of laboratory schools serving as subject pools for externally driven research projects (McBride et al., 2012) would not be appropriate as a framework guiding such a consortium. The field of "Applied Developmental Science" (ADS) provides valuable insight into a vision for laboratory schools as they strive to identify new conceptual models that will guide efforts for the creation of a consortium.

ADS is "scholarship that seeks to advance the integration of developmental research with actions—policies and programs—that promote positive development and/or enhance the life chances of vulnerable children and families" (Lerner, Fisher, & Weinberg, 2000, p. 11). ADS "has its roots in numerous fields concerned with human development" (Lerner, Jacobs, & Wertlieb, 2005, p. 4) including home economics, human ecology, family and consumer sciences, comparative psychology, and developmental psychology. A laboratory school consortium built upon developmental research from transdisciplinary perspectives represented in fields such as these can play a critical role in addressing the disconnect among theory, research, and practice in the early childhood field.

Creation of a consortium built upon an ADS framework can be an important first step in positioning laboratory schools at the forefront of efforts to generate new knowledge that can guide both policy and practice through the generation of new insight on factors that contribute to young children's early learning and development (McBride et al., 2012). Several objectives can be achieved as a result of the creation of such a consortium whereby laboratory schools would combine their efforts in joint and reciprocal research and teacher training activities, including the following:

- facilitation of an interdisciplinary and transdisciplinary approach to translational research;
- creation of mechanisms to overcome historical constraints on the utility of knowledge being generated in laboratory school settings;
- facilitation of research that utilizes protocols more difficult to implement in community-based settings;
- implementation of activities that can directly inform policy decisions;
- replication and economies of scale resulting from multi-site data collection;
- creation of diversity in data collection processes (e.g. populations served, geographic settings, program models, etc.);
- facilitation of research that is responsive to the needs of the early childhood field;
- implementation of data collection protocols designed to address difficult problems not easily addressed.

As being proposed by several authors in this edited volume, a consortium that draws upon an applied developmental sciences paradigm, and that links several university laboratory schools for joint and reciprocal data collection and teacher training efforts, would require careful consideration of critical data and infrastructure needs that would be necessary in order to allow such an initiative to address the objectives outlined above. The purpose of this chapter is to provide a context for initial discussions on how these data and infrastructure needs could be developed and implemented within a laboratory school consortium framework. Insight from the lessons learned in the revitalization of the Child Development Laboratory (CDL) program on the University of Illinois at Urbana/Champaign campus will be used to provide a context that guides discussions on the development of this data and infrastructure framework (Branscomb & McBride, 2005).

Child Development Laboratory—University of Illinois at Urbana/Champaign

The Child Development Laboratory (CDL) program on the campus of the University of Illinois at Urbana/Champaign (UIUC) has a rich, 74-year history of facilitating teaching, research and outreach activities of faculty, staff, and students on the UIUC campus. Through the years the CDL has established an infrastructure for facilitating research projects while at the same time providing high quality early childhood services for enrolled children. Although the CDL consistently served as a supportive arena for conducting research, it wasn't until the implementation of the CDL Research Database Project (RDP) that such efforts moved beyond one-time data collection efforts. These one-time projects were completed on a semester/yearly basis with little or no cross-communication between investigators or systematic compilation of data. Such an approach failed to capitalize on the shared research interests and expertise of faculty within the UIUC, and limited the ability of the CDL to facilitate a programmatic research agenda designed to address important developmental issues facing children and their families.

Since its inception in 1998, the implementation of the CDL RDP has played a significant role in shaping the nature of the research being conducted at the program. As a result of the resources provided through the database project, many of the studies being implemented at the CDL now take an ADS approach to data collection, and capitalize on the reciprocal exchange of data that is made available to investigators implementing projects. In doing so, research projects coming through the CDL will often address the three conjoint emphases underlying ADS—those being, 1. research that is *applied* with direct implications for children, families, practitioners, and policymakers; 2. research that is *developmental* in how they relate to systematic and successive changes within human systems; and 3. research that is considered *science*-based on its grounding in robust research methods (Lerner et al., 2005). This has allowed researchers to develop a more comprehensive approach to generating data on the topics which they are investigating while expanding the types of data available for use in their projects, thus enhancing the types of questions they are able to address in their studies. Exploration of the data and infrastructure components that have allowed the CDL RDP to have a significant impact on the research and teaching activities emerging from the UIUC campus can be an important first step in the effort to create a university-based laboratory school consortium.

Data and Infrastructure Needs of a Laboratory School Consortium

Data Needs

A major goal for the creation of a consortium being discussed as part of this book is to link laboratory schools at multiple institutions for joint and reciprocal research data collection and teacher training projects. A core infrastructure component that would be critical in facilitating such activities would be creating systems within the participating institutions for the gathering, organizing, storing, managing, and sharing of data collected as part of consortium initiatives. The CDL RDP at the University of Illinois provides a starting point for developing a working model for what such a database management system might look like within a laboratory school consortium model.

As part of the CDL RDP, extensive data is gathered each year on all children enrolled in the program (i.e. 160 children, ages 6 weeks to 5 years). This data comes from multiple sources (i.e. parental reports, teacher reports, direct observations and assessments), and draws upon both validated measurement tools as well as instruments developed specifically for the RDP. Information gathered as part of the RDP focuses on a wide range of constructs that are of interest to researchers who utilize enrolled children and their families as participants in their studies, including:

- basic family demographic data (e.g. parent age; parent education; parental employment status; household composition, etc.);
- extensive parental reports on child information (e.g. age; gender; general health history and current health status; sleep patterns; friendship patterns and peer networks; non-parental care history, etc.);
- data on family routines and parenting styles;
- parent and teacher reports on child characteristics (e.g. temperament, behavior, etc.);
- parent and teacher reports on child interests;
- direct assessments of the child's developmental status using standardized screening tools (i.e. Bayley Infant Neurodevelopmental Screener (BINS) for infants and toddlers, and the DENVER II developmental screener for older children).

Much of the parental report data comes from information gathered from parents at the beginning of each school/enrollment year using web-based survey tools, while teacher report and direct assessment data is gathered during the fall semester of each school/enrollment year. All data collected as part of the RDP is compiled in a master database, which is then made available for researchers and instructors accessing enrolled children and their families as part of their research or teaching activities.

Strengths of the RDP Approach

There are several factors which have contributed to the success of the RDP that have direct relevance to the data and infrastructure needs of a laboratory school consortium. The most salient of these factors is the ongoing nature of the information that is contained in the RDP database. The RDP has become a longitudinal database consisting of normative data on children's social, motor, language, and cognitive development as they progress through the CDL program from infancy until they make the transition to kindergarten. This web-based data source plays an important role for both historical and projective analyses as part of research being conducted on the UIUC laboratory school with respect to child-, family-, and education-related outcomes.

A second major strength of the RDP approach for compiling information is its ability to minimize respondent burdens placed on parents/families of children participating in studies. The CDL program facilitates 25–30 research projects each year. These projects are initiated by investigators from a wide range of departmental and disciplinary backgrounds, and involve diverse methodological approaches for data collection. In spite of the diversity reflected in the methodological approaches being used in studies conducted at the CDL, most projects gathering data on enrolled children and their families are interested in the same types of demographic data on their participants (e.g. child age and gender; parental age, education, and employment status; family SES; family household composition, etc.). Having this information contained in the RDP database negates the need for each research team to ask parents/families for the same types of information. Having such information readily available in the database also streamlines the data collection process for research teams, and insures consistency in how this information is compiled across projects. This information also simplifies the process of identifying potential participants for research studies. For example, if an investigator is interested in assessing language styles of all children ages 24 to 36 months who have an older sibling between the ages of 36 and 60 months, a quick query of specific fields in the database can yield a list of all children who meet these parameters.

A third major strength of the RDP approach for compiling information is its ability to enhance the knowledge being developed as part of individual studies through the reciprocal exchange of data across projects. As part of the RDP protocol, an initial meeting between the CDL Director and investigators interested in collecting data at the program is held to discuss various aspects of the research process. One part of this discussion is to explore the potential of projects sharing data with the RDP for use with future studies. For example, a recent project at the CDL focused on children's peer relationships within classroom contexts. One measure used for data collection was the Behavior Problem Index (BPI), a commonly used tool to assess preschool teachers' perceptions of children's externalizing behavior problems. The lead investigator for this project agreed to allow children's BPI ratings to be added to the research database for use with future studies. Future studies that are conducted at the CDL will then have access to this behavioral problems data without having the need to actually collect the information. Although it may not have been part of the original research design, these future studies may wish to include perceived behavior problems as an important construct to include in the conceptual and data analytic plan as they attempt to examine the correlates/determinants of the phenomenon the new studies are addressing, thus enhancing the knowledge being generated. It should be noted that not all research projects taking place at the CDL gather data for which sharing with the RDP would make sense (e.g. a study of the coordination of respiration and swallowing processes in children with sensory processing disorders). Similarly, some investigators gathering data at the CDL may have constraints (e.g. funding source guidelines; use of proprietary measures, etc.) that limit their ability to share data with the RDP. In spite of these constraints, the potential benefits to a laboratory school consortium that could result from the reciprocal exchange of data with the database are significant, and provide a major source of justification for the creation of a laboratory school consortium model.

A fourth strength resulting from the use of a research database approach within a laboratory school consortium framework would come from the economies of scale and potential diversity in subject pools achieved by collecting common data across sites participating in the consortium. One limitation of conducting research within laboratory school settings is the limited size of enrollments in such programs. Although the CDL program at the University of Illinois is relatively large and enrolls 160 children, ages 6 weeks to 5 years, this is still a small "n," especially when examining subgroups within the program (e.g. only 24 infants between 6 weeks to 12 months). Expanding data collection across multiple laboratory schools participating within the consortium significantly expands the potential subject pool for studies being conducted, and can add much needed statistical power for data analyses. For example, a recent pilot study was conducted at the CDL that focused on infants' reaction to verbal comments during mealtimes as the babies transitioned from breast milk or formula to table foods and solids. Over the course of an enrollment year this research team was able to gather data on this transition process with 17 of the infants enrolled in the program—the other 7 babies in the infant classrooms had already transitioned to table foods prior to being enrolled in the program. Although an n of 17 was appropriate for this pilot study designed to explore the feasibility of a new data collection protocol, such small sample sizes are problematic for many research studies. Having a data collection protocol which could be implemented across multiple laboratory schools would provide sufficient sample sizes and power in the analyses to allow the study to make definitive conclusions about the phenomena being examined—e.g. babies' responses to verbal comments made during mealtimes as they transition to solid foods. Gathering data at multiple laboratory school sites also enhances the potential diversity that is present in the subject pool (e.g. child race/ethnicity, family SES, etc.).

A final strength that could result from the use of a research database approach within a laboratory school consortium framework would be its ability to combine teaching and research activities at each of the participating laboratory schools. For example, baseline developmental data is gathered at the beginning of each enrollment year for children attending the CDL program. As part of this process, advanced undergraduate students enrolled in an assessment class at the University of Illinois spend the fall semester learning about strengths and limitations of standardized assessment tools for use with young children, as well as the appropriate and inappropriate use of such tools. As part of this course they are also trained on conducting child screenings using the Bayley Infant Neurodevelopmental Screener (BINS) for infants and toddlers, and the DENVER II developmental screener for older children. Once trained on these tools, they are assigned to conduct screenings on 10–12 children enrolled in the CDL program. Results from these screenings are then shared with parents and teachers, while the information is also added to the RDP for research projects. This approach adds valuable information to the data made available for researchers while at the same time addressing the professional development needs of university students pursuing career paths that might require them to have a working knowledge of standardized assessments with young children.

Critical Questions with an RDP Approach

Although the use of a Research Database Project (RDP) method to implement reciprocal and joint data collection ventures across multiple sites would greatly enhance the productivity of a proposed laboratory school consortium, such an approach raises several challenging issues and questions. Effectively answering these questions would be critical to the overall success of a laboratory school consortium that would utilize an RDP approach. Additionally, addressing these critical questions will be an important first step in allowing a laboratory school consortium to tackle head on a major premise underlying the ADS perspective as outlined by Lerner and colleagues (Lerner et al., 2005)—that is, creating a mechanism by which developmental scientists can play a meaningful role in tackling society's urgent problems related to children, families, and communities.

What are the Major Functions of a Database System for a Laboratory School Consortium?

Although the answer to this question appears obvious at first, the potential range of responses can play an important role in shaping how a laboratory school consortium is implemented, as well as dictating its purpose and function. For example, if the primary goal of a laboratory school consortium is to increase the size of subject pools for data collection, the main functions of an RDP would be to warehouse data for analyses. In contrast, if the goal of the consortium is to create a system for facilitating innovative approaches to generating new knowledge via joint and reciprocal data collection protocols, the functions and structure of the RDP would be very different.

Which Clientele Groups will have Access to Information Contained in the RDP, both within Participating Laboratory Schools, and Across Institutions?

There are several different directions the issue of access to RDP data could adapt, each of which would take initiatives within the laboratory school consortium in different directions. For example, restricting access to RDP data to staff affiliated with the respective laboratory schools would significantly limit the types of activities that might be implemented as part of the consortium, and would result in a narrow range of projects being implemented that are reflective of the expertise represented in the small number of laboratory school staff that have a research focus. In contrast, if access to information in the RDP is granted to researchers conducting studies as part of the consortium (i.e. individual investigator at one institution proposes a study that is then implemented across all sites participating in the consortium), the range of topics being addressed in the consortium and methodologies being used as part of research activities would be greatly expanded. Such an approach would also enhance and expand the knowledge being generated via consortium research activities.

A third alternative to the issue of access would be to create systems that would allow investigators from institutions participating in the laboratory school consortium who are not collecting original data to have access to RDP data for secondary data analysis. Creating an RDP longitudinal database of normative data on children's social, motor, language, and cognitive development as part of a laboratory school consortium would provide a potentially rich source of information that could be used to inform historical and projective analyses across a wide range of topics. Although a more challenging approach, the potential of such a strategy for granting access to the RDP for secondary data analysis projects to significantly expand the types of knowledge being generated as part of the consortium activities is enormous.

Closely related to the issue of access to the RDP database for secondary data analysis is graduate and undergraduate student access to the data. It is conceivable that a consortium RDP database would provide a rich source of information for students to use as part of research methods class projects, or for theses and dissertations. Students often do not have the funding or time resources that would allow them to collect original data for such projects. Having access to data in a consortium RDP database could expand the options available to them for such work.

What Levels of Data would be Available within the RDP?

Discussions on the types of data that would be available as part of an RDP database would need to be addressed early in the planning process for creating a laboratory school consortium. Decisions on the types of data that would be gathered (e.g. family demographic data, direct developmental assessment data, teacher and parental report data, etc.), as well as how decisions related to the reciprocal exchanges of data would be handled, will be critical to the overall success of the laboratory consortium. The richer the data contained in the RDP database, the more attractive the laboratory consortium will be for researchers and instructors.

How will Institutional Review Board (IRB) Approval be Addressed for Multi-site Data Collection

Each laboratory school participating in the proposed consortium will be operating under IRB approval systems that are unique to their respective institutions. Reciprocity in IRB approval (i.e. an investigator at one institution receives IRB approval for a data collection protocol that would then be implemented at all sites participating in the consortium) across institutions cannot be assumed. Although reciprocity in IRB approval across institutions would be ideal, past history with research projects emerging from the CDL at the University of Illinois that involved data collection at other institutions suggests this is unlikely. Given this, the goal may be to work toward all institutions participating in the consortium having a "memorandum of understanding" (MOU) in which research protocols that are initiated and have been granted IRB approval at one institution would receive "expedited" IRB reviews at all other institutions in the consortium. Regardless of what systems are ultimately in place for IRB approval of consortium data collection initiatives, investigators need to be advised that they should address IRB-related issues early in the planning process for projects to be implemented as part of the laboratory school consortium.

Infrastructure Needs

Although the creation of an RDP database would support activities emerging from a laboratory school consortium, the database itself will not insure success of the consortium initiative. Several different infrastructure components will be needed that would support the RDP database and related initiatives in order to increase the ability of the consortium to achieve its stated goals. The following is a partial listing of what these infrastructure needs might be.

Consortium Advisory Committee

The creation of an advisory committee will be critical in guiding the development, implementation and evaluation of a multisite laboratory school consortium. Members of this advisory committee should represent the various stakeholders who might be involved in consortium activities (e.g. laboratory school administrators, laboratory school teachers, university instructors, researchers, campus administrators, parents of enrolled children, etc.). Advisory committee members should also be cognizant of the demands associated with balancing academic, research, and service needs within a laboratory school classroom context. This advisory committee would be charged with developing a "shared" vision for the laboratory school consortium goals and objectives, as well as the mechanisms that will need to be in place to insure progress is made toward reaching these goals and objectives. This committee would also be charged with developing the tools and protocols that would be used to monitor and evaluate the progress of consortium activities, and then using such tools to guide the iterative process of developing a true laboratory school consortium.

Web-based Tools for Submitting Consortium Requests

A laboratory school consortium committed to facilitating joint and reciprocal research and instructional projects that will be implemented across multiple sites will need mechanisms for fielding requests from investigators and instructors at institutions participating in the consortium. As part of its own Research Database Project (RDP), the Child Development Laboratory (CDL) at the University of Illinois has a web-based tool used by investigators to submit research requests for collecting data with CDL teachers, enrolled children, and their families. This web-based *CDL Research Request* form requires investigators to provide several key pieces of information regarding their proposed studies (e.g. demographic and contact information of the investigator; research questions to be addressed; target populations and/or classrooms; overview of methodologies to be used; timeline for implementation of the project; key personnel involved; and specific information on IRB approval). This form is not meant to place an additional burden on the research teams submitting the request, so it is designed to only elicit the level of detail needed to evaluate the feasibility of the protocols being proposed. It does NOT require the level of detail you would see in research grant proposals or journal articles in terms of methodologies, samples, etc. Once submitted, this *CDL Research Request* form is automatically sent to the email in-box of members of the standing committee that reviews such requests. In addition, information from the form is also automatically dumped into a database that is then used to track the various research studies that take place each year. A similar web-based *CDL Class Project and Observations* form is used to field requests from students/ instructors wanting to conduct classroom observations (e.g. observations of children's motor skills as part of a weekly lab for a kinesiology class) or classroom projects (e.g. language assessments of children) as part of requirements for courses at the university. The *CDL Research Request* form and the *CDL Class Project and Observations* form have proven to be valuable management tools that have allowed the CDL to effectively facilitate and track 25–30 research projects, 3,500–4,000 student observations, and 1,500–1,750 class projects on an annual basis. Similar web-based tools will be critical for successfully facilitating and tracking research and teaching activities being implemented at multiple sites participating in the proposed laboratory school consortium.

Recruitment/Marketing of the Laboratory School Consortium to Academic Communities at Participating Institutions

If implemented correctly, a laboratory school consortium committed to facilitating joint and reciprocal data collection and instructional projects across multiple sites could become a valuable resource for researchers and instructors at the participating institutions. This will only become a reality though if researchers and instructors at the participating institutions are aware of the resources provided by the consortium, and are informed of the procedures required to get projects approved for implementation. As such, recruitment and marketing initiatives that target the academic communities at participating institutions and communicate the resources and opportunities available via the laboratory school consortium will need to be developed. As part of the initial phase of the launch of the RDP at the CDL at the University of Illinois in 1998, a concerted 2-year campus-wide marketing campaign was undertaken by the Director to inform the academic community on the campus of the resources available through the initiative. This marketing campaign took several formats (e.g. presentations at graduate research seminar classes; presentations at departmental research seminars; broad distribution of print and electronic documents outlining resources available through the RDP; one-on-one consultations with researchers and instructors; conducting "open house" events for the academic community, etc.). Regardless of the format of these marketing efforts, the content in the message being communicated was the same—that is, the structure/nature of the CDL program and the RDP; an overview of the goals and objectives of the RDP; a description of the resources available to researchers and instructors from the RDP; and an overview of why the CDL program and its RDP are attractive for researchers and instructors. Since the initial launch of the RDP, a series of web-based materials has been developed that provides the University of Illinois academic community with similar kinds of information, including an overview of the RDP at the CDL, an overview of research and teaching activities taking place at the CDL, an overview of the policies and procedures that guide implementation of research and teaching activities, a listing of resources available for teaching and research activities, and a "virtual tour" of how research and teaching activities are implemented at the CDL. This web-based information, combined with the annual open house event each spring for the academic community, continues to provide excellent mechanisms for marketing the CDL program as a viable site for conducting research and teaching activities. Similar marketing efforts will need to be developed to insure the success of the proposed laboratory school consortium.

Protocols for Screening and Managing Proposed Data Collection/Teaching Projects

The old adage "build it and they shall come" should serve as a cautionary tale that informs the creation of a laboratory school consortium. In order for the proposed consortium to become a valuable resource for instructors and researchers, clearly articulated policies and procedures will need to be in place prior to the actual launching of the initiative. These policies and procedures would outline screening and approval processes for research and teaching activities that would be implemented across the participating sites. Having such policies and procedures clearly articulated for the academic community is one factor that has contributed to the success of the CDL RDP. All research and teaching requests are screened by a standing committee made up of the CDL Director, CDL Associate Director, one CDL lead teacher, and one faculty member from the department in which the CDL is housed. This screening process does not evaluate the quality of the science of the research or the pedagogy of the teaching activities being proposed. Instead, all requests are screened to judge the feasibility of the methods/activities being proposed within the constraints of the CDL context. There is an explicit set of criteria that is used to screen the research and teaching requests that are communicated to investigators and instructors at multiple points during the implementation process (e.g. in the "policies" section of the CDL website for researchers and instructors; in written documentation that is provided to researchers and instructors; in initial interactions between the CDL Director and researchers or instructors, etc.). The goal of this screening process is to not say "NO" to a research or teaching request, but instead to work with the investigators and instructors to identify ways in which their work can be successfully implemented within the constraints of the CDL program. Similar screening and approval protocols will need to be developed for the proposed laboratory school consortium to insure transparency is evident in how consortium activities are identified and implemented across participating institutions.

Closely related to the development of project screening and approval protocols is the need to develop mechanisms within the proposed laboratory school consortium for managing the potential influx of new research and teaching activities. One immediate challenge that emerged with the implementation of the CDL RDP at the University of Illinois was the significant increase in the number of researchers and instructors seeking to implement projects at the program. Like most laboratory school programs, the CDL is limited in the number of children, families, teachers, classrooms, and research spaces that are available to support research and teaching activities. Because of this limitation, specific protocols and tools had to be developed to manage the new influx of projects being implemented (e.g. master planning calendars for classrooms and research spaces; guidelines for advanced scheduling of project implementation; protocols for communicating upcoming research and teaching activities to teachers and families; criteria for managing overlapping teaching and research activities with teacher planned classroom activities, etc.). A major goal for the use of these protocols and tools has been to create a climate where the needs of researchers and instructors will be met while at the same time balancing these activities with the needs of enrolled children and their teachers. Similar protocols and tools will need to be developed to manage the potential influx of activities that would occur at laboratory schools participating in the proposed consortium.

Training Mechanisms to Support Joint and Reciprocal Research and Teaching Activities

One goal of the proposed laboratory school consortium would be to have a variety of research and teaching initiatives emerge from individual institutions that are then implemented across all laboratory schools participating in the consortium. It is probable that the types of research and teaching activities that will emerge from this initiative will involve a wide range of methodologies and strategies. Training will be critical if these activities are to be successfully implemented across participating sites. An important component of the CDL RDP at the University of Illinois is its emphasis on providing training to the various constituent groups involved in research and teaching activities. This training takes on several different formats depending on the focus of the projects being implemented (e.g. training of teachers during a staff meeting on how to implement a teaching strategy that is being evaluated as part of a study; training undergraduate research assistants on protocols for use when collecting data with children at the CDL; training teachers on how to use an "event sampling" data recording tool as part of a research study; training research assistants working with investigators on the unique aspects of collecting data from children attending CDL classrooms, etc.). The doctoral student assigned to the RDP works with researchers and instructors implementing projects at the CDL, and then coordinates the requisite training for identified targets on an as-needed basis. Although the replication of these training efforts will be challenging when working with teachers and staff at multiple sites, the use of web-based tools and webinar formats will ease the implementation of such efforts with laboratory schools participating in the consortium.

Financial Support for Laboratory School Consortium Activities

Implementation of research and teaching activities within a laboratory school context requires facility, human, and financial resources for successful execution. Most laboratory schools have the physical facilities in place to conduct research and teaching activities (e.g. observation booths into classrooms; pull-out rooms for data collection with children, etc.). Most programs also have the human resources needed to facilitate such activities (e.g. well-trained teachers who implement "model" programming within their classrooms; staff members committed to the lab school model of generating new knowledge; administrators versed in balancing the needs of researchers and instructors with those of enrolled children and their teachers, etc.). What is often missing though in many laboratory school programs is the financial resources needed to support the implementation of research and teaching activities.

Financial support has been one of the major contributors to the success of the CDL RDP at the University of Illinois. Departmental, college, and campus financial support was secured early on in the planning process for the implementation of the RDP, with the majority of this support coming from the Office of the Provost (OP) and the Office of the Vice-Chancellor for Research (OVCR). The CDL RDP was developed as a "campus-level" resource that would provide the infrastructure needed to enhance a wide variety of research and teaching initiatives emerging from researchers and instructors from across campus. This is in contrast to what occurs with many laboratory schools that are viewed as primarily a departmental-level resource. With campus-level funds received through indirect cost recovery (ICR) monies generated on externally funded grants, a recurring budget line-item is funneled from the OP and OVCR to the CDL budget to support the RDP activities. In comparison to support provided for other research and teaching infrastructures on campus, the monies provided to the CDL RDP are relatively small (i.e. equivalent of a 0.50 FTE 12-month research assistantship appointment plus monies to cover costs of research materials). The return on this small investment is significant though in terms of increased research and teaching productivity being generated as a result of CDL RDP activities (e.g. increase in external grants being funded as a result of data collected at the CDL). Using a similar approach at institutions participating in the proposed laboratory school consortium (i.e. presenting the consortium as a "campus-level" infrastructure support that will provide a return on the investment) may be an effective approach to garnering the financial support that will be needed to successfully implement consortium activities.

Mechanisms for the Dissemination of Consortium Activities

Dissemination of consortium activities will be crucial for the sustainability of the initiative, especially if campus buy-in (conceptually and financially) is necessary for its implementation. Administrators at institutions participating in the consortium will need to know what the return will be from supporting such an initiative for their respective universities. The *CDL Annual Report* provides one model for what this dissemination format might take. The *CDL Annual Report* is a document generated each year and outlines the various ways in which the CDL program supports research and teaching activities. It compiles a detailed listing of each research project conducted (e.g. study name; investigator(s) and affiliations; questions being addressed; target CDL populations used, etc.), a detailed listing of each university course that was supported for classroom observations along with the number of students and contact hours spent at the CDL as part of the observations, and a detailed listing of the class projects implemented along with the university course the projects were used to support and the number of students from the course. The resulting report is a data driven document that clearly articulates the multitude of ways in which the academic and scholarly activities of students, instructors, and researchers were supported during the past year by the CDL. Each year a copy of the *CDL Annual Report* is sent to department heads, deans, and associate deans from units on campus that had students or faculty implementing activities at the CDL, as well as several campus-level administrators (i.e. Provost, Vice Chancellor for Research, etc.). In receiving this document the administrators are able to see firsthand how their faculty and students have benefited from the academic activities supported by the CDL. Such an approach provides a powerful tool for communicating to campus-level administrators what the return is on their investments in the CDL RDP. A similar approach for disseminating activities from the proposed laboratory school consortium will be instrumental in insuring its long-term sustainability.

Conclusions

The description above of data and infrastructure needs for a proposed laboratory school consortium is just a partial listing of those factors that will need to be addressed in order to insure the success of such an initiative. Developing, implementing, and evaluating the impact of a laboratory school consortium based on an ADS perspective should be viewed as an iterative process, with many of the tools and processes necessary for the success of such an initiative not known until the planning and implementation process is well under way. In spite of this uncertainty, creation of a laboratory school consortium is a goal our field should be moving toward. As mentioned earlier, there is an increasing gap between theory, research, and practice in the child development and early childhood education fields. The creation of a proposed laboratory school consortium that draws from an applied developmental sciences framework, such as the one being discussed in this volume, can become an important first step in positioning laboratory schools at the forefront of efforts to address, and ultimately reduce, this gap. As described by McBride and his colleagues (McBride et al., 2012), laboratory schools should be viewed as providing models for discovery and knowledge generation. The creation of a consortium with the accompanying data and infrastructure supports described in this chapter will take this model of knowledge generation to an important and much needed next level. In doing so a laboratory school consortium can assume a leadership role in addressing the overarching goal of ADS as outlined by Lerner and colleagues (Lerner et al., 2000)—that is, to create a context of scholarship that advances the integration of developmental research with policies and programs that promote positive development for children and families.

References

Branscomb, K. R., & McBride, B. A. (2005). Academics versus service: Balancing competing missions in laboratory schools offering full-day programming. *Journal of Early Childhood Teacher Education, 25*, 113–121.

Elicker, J., & Barbour, N. (2015). *University laboratory preschools.* Oxford, UK: Routledge.

Hustedt, J. T., & Barnett, W. S. (2011). Financing early childhood education programs: State, federal, and local issues. *Educational Policy, 25*, 167–192.

Lerner, R. M., Fisher, C. B., & Weinberg, R. A. (2000). Toward a science for and of the people: Promoting civil society through the application of developmental science. *Child Development, 71*, 11–20.

Lerner, R. M., Jacobs, F., & Wertlieb, D. (2005). *Applied Developmental Science: An advanced textbook.* Thousand Oaks, CA: Sage.

McBride, B. A., Groves, M., Barbour, N., Horm, D., Stremmel, A., Lash, M., Bersani, C., Ratekin, C., Moran, J., Elicker, J., & Toussaint, S. (2012). Child Development Laboratory schools as generators of knowledge in early childhood education: New models and approaches. *Early Education and Development, 23*(2), 153–164.

Pungello, E. P., Kainz, K., Burchinal, M., Wasik, B. H., Sparling, J. J., Ramey, C. T., & Campbell, F. A. (2010). Early educational intervention, early cumulative risk, and the early home environment as predictors of young adult outcomes within a high-risk sample. *Child Development, 81*, 410–426.

Sabol, T. J., & Pianta, R. C. (2012). Patterns of school readiness forecast achievement and socioemotional development at the end of elementary school. *Child Development, 83*, 282–289.

Saracho, O. N., & Spodek, B. (2012). *Handbook of research on the education of young children* (3rd ed.). New York: Routledge.

Thompson, R. (2002). Set for success: Building a strong foundation for school readiness based on the social-emotional development of young children. *The Kauffman Early Education Exchange, 1*, 8–29.

3

EXPANDING RESEARCH FROM COLLABORATIVE SELF-STUDY TO AN APPLIED DEVELOPMENTAL SCIENCE MODEL

Martha Lash and Monica Miller Marsh

This chapter reflects and shares the Kent State University Child Development Center's (CDC) university lab school's examination and recalibration of their three-pronged mission of teaching, service, and research. More specifically, it examines the role and type of research conducted at the CDC and strives to address how the recalibrated perspectives potentially align with an Applied Developmental Science (ADS) model [More explicit definitions of ADS provided elsewhere in this volume]. The CDC, founded in 1972, is a nationally recognized laboratory school that has played a central role in serving young children and families, engaging in professional development of pre- and in-service teachers, and generating research to inform practice. The CDC theoretical base is social constructivism and posits that knowledge is constructed through an active process of exploring, investigating, and playing. The curriculum, inspired by the Reggio Emilia (RE) approach (Edwards, Gandini, & Forman, 2011), is based on the belief that every child is capable and competent. Recently, the CDC has become an International Baccalaurate Primary Years Programme Candidate School (IBO.org) with inquiry as a learning approach.

A snapshot of the CDC shows that it serves 150 children and families from ten countries, has eight classrooms for children, an extensive outdoor learning lab, and a college classroom for teaching early childhood education majors. The CDC encourages research that is collaborative and classroom-based, as children's learning in their environments is a first priority. In terms of educational background of the teachers and leadership team, all of the nine master teachers have had experiences with reading and reviewing research, writing papers, and conducting small scale research projects. The master teachers, the Outdoor Educator, and the Family Services Coordinator all hold master's degrees and the Studio Teacher holds a doctorate; additionally, unique to this laboratory school is that the master teachers and the Outdoor Educator are full-time positions (family services coordinator and studio teacher are part-time). Of the three part-time administrators, one holds a master's degree and two hold doctorates. Pre-service teachers are in classrooms for field and student teaching experiences and are not counted in the teacher–child ratios. Spanning several years, and until 2012 when there was a leadership change, the CDC articulated that approved research must feature the CDC teachers engaging in ongoing inquiry into their own practices. In hindsight, this clearly limited the research conducted, replication possibilities, and research presentations and publications. What was intended as a protection for children's ongoing school experience became a limitation for the CDC to reach its full capacity as a laboratory school. While the CDC aligns with the teacher education laboratory school model, the expectations for research in child development and/or teacher education were restricted by their own pre-2012 guidelines.

We examined and critiqued how the CDC evolved from a teacher inquiry and collaborative self-study model of research into one that builds upon this history to include making their research public. As the CDC and its teachers and administrators transitioned to a research model that extended beyond teacher action research, we wrestled with many important questions. What do we mean by inquiry? What does it mean to do research? How does teacher action research compare with research conducted by those other than employees at the CDC? This process then evolved into more ethical and research-focused queries. What does it mean to collaborate in research? Who "holds" the research that happens in classrooms with an inquiry-based program? Who is allowed to decide if and how a classroom inquiry is made public? Who is responsible and credited for writing up the shared research? What are the risks associated with moving from internal teacher action research and reflection to complete the final research step of making the work public—open for inspection and replication? Questions surrounding, defining, and understanding what it means to inquire and to conduct research are essential questions in every program and these proved to be paramount for the CDC.

Thus, the invitation to be part of a larger consortium that wanted to share lab school research in an applied developmental science (ADS) model, during and shortly after a lab school change in leadership, brought these essential questions to the forefront. As a result of these questions, there have been dialogue, exploration, and implementation of various research practices, and an unequivocal articulation of the need to join in with such efforts of a consortium to stay current, intelligently anticipate the future, and to be viable as a lab school.

This chapter highlights two key components of the Kent State University (KSU) Child Development Center (CDC) lab school in relation to its participation in a Lab School Consortium adhering to an ADS Model: 1) How does the teacher-as-researcher model in collaborative projects support the ADS Model? and 2) How does the ADS perspective inform efforts to reshape/expand the paradigms guiding activities in the lab school? (McBride et al., 2012). And, in so doing, how does the CDC provide a research site that attends to all components of our mission—teaching, service, and our recalibrated emphasis on research that aligns with university laboratory school expectations? (Elicker & Barbour, 2012; File, 2012).

Conducting an inventory of our past and current efforts at the CDC was an important process and acknowledgment as we made a commitment to moving forward. This reflective inventory showed that our pre-2012 research revealed self-study and beginning collaboration, which leaned toward the ADS model (i.e. direct implications, development across the lifespan). This process also calls upon us to ask how our many efforts and labor-intensive work are reflected in research outcomes such as presentations, publications, and theory-to-practice applications. Evidence of these practices and research efforts, many of which showed initial alignment with the ADS model (i.e. direct implications, reciprocity), are visible in the CDC's research, including collaborating with other RE-inspired programs in study groups and in cross-site research with other RE-inspired laboratory schools. These teacher collaborative research partnerships include 1) South Dakota State University (SDSU) for self-study of teacher professional development and study of children's small group work (Cutler et al., 2012); and 2) Prairie Partners collaboration (including KSU, SDSU, and University of Nebraska), which involved three lab schools jointly developing, piloting, and revising a classroom child observation tool to be used by pre-service teachers for honing observation skills. Additionally, many local partnerships within the University and greater local Kent communities had been forged to promote emerging curricula (e.g. master gardeners, fraternities, national park). As we delved into our recent history, we noted these strides were valuable for curriculum and reflection, but they rarely resulted in publications, impact on practice, and research-oriented presentations.

Moving Toward an ADS Model

Miller Marsh (one of the co-authors), a graduate of the Kent State University Early Childhood Education program, who completed her student teaching and a semester-long substitute kindergarten teaching position at the Child Development Center in the late 1980s, is an advocate of laboratory schools and the ADS model. Prior to accepting the Directorship at the Child Development Center, Miller Marsh taught at a small private university in Pennsylvania, a state in which laboratory schools were at risk. The laboratory school affiliated with Pennsylvania State University was outsourced to Hildebrandt Learning Centers (now known as Bright Horizons) and the lab school connected to the Community College with whom she worked was outsourced a short time later. Her commitment to the mission of laboratory schools, which she describes as studying the relationship of educational theories to best practices, preparing teachers based on these findings, and disseminating information, was the main reason she pursued the position at Kent State.

One of the things she found most challenging as the newly hired director of the Child Development Center and early childhood faculty was that the teachers at the CDC had been engaging in labor-intensive inquiry-oriented work with children, parents, prospective teachers, and their colleagues for years but the work was not being shared with a more public audience. There were mounds of documentation/data piled up and locked away in a documentation lab that were rarely used. Working alongside Child Development Center faculty and staff, Miller Marsh generated some new ways to support moving teachers' work into the public realm as well as opening the doors to other researchers.

In order to work toward the goal of completing the research cycle, which meant moving beyond the more self-contained teacher action research and moving forward to research shared in a public forum, the CDC teachers and administrative and pedagogical leaders needed to embrace a model or models where colleagues and/or other university personnel could support one another throughout the research process. In this process, the CDC realized their teacher action research processes, when completed, were very much synchronized with the ADS tenet that ADS is reciprocal—science drives application and application drives science (Lerner, Wertlieb, & Jacobs, 2005). Three exploratory models of research were devised and implemented at this time, namely, the CDC Team Approach, the Participatory Action Research Approach, and the summer STEAM Camp Approach. Explanations of each of the models and examples are given in the following three sections.

Exploratory Model One: CDC Team Approach

The CDC faculty decided to form four small groups to support the work that was being studied and documented by four lead classroom teachers. This way the faculty would be working together to support research that was already in progress. For example, two of the research groups focused on the Outdoor Learning Laboratory (OLL). The creation of the OLL had been a dream of the school community for many years. Teachers, parents, and children had been imagining what a new outdoor space could look like prior to the OLL being funded by the university. Documentation existed of the meetings in which parents and faculty discussed their ideas for the outdoors as well as faculty meeting minutes in which teachers had shared their ideas and drawn up plans detailing possibilities for the large outdoor space. In addition, teachers had recorded children's ideas and documented their play behaviors on the current space.

Given that there was much data already gathered on this project and we could move quickly into the analysis phase, it made sense for one group to focus on this topic and move it toward publication. The team formed for this particular research project entitled, *"I Would Change the Classroom and Put It Out There": The Design and Development of an Outdoor Learning Laboratory*, consisted of one administrator and three teachers. The specific aim of this research was to illustrate how the perspectives of teachers, parents, and children were integrated into the design of our new outdoor space.

The Kent State University Child Development Center is fortunate to be located on the path of a hike and bike trail that winds around a designated wetlands area. A large part of the curriculum emerges from the children's experiences during their hikes into "the meadow." One of the concerns that emerged for the teachers as the OLL was being constructed was that a more open outdoor space around the school could change the types of experiences children had in the meadow. Teachers even wondered in some of the earlier discussions if they or the children would be reluctant to leave the OLL when so much was available to them right around our school. Based on these questions and concerns, a second research team was formed to conduct a study entitled, *Listening to Preschool Children's Perspectives: A Comparison of Play Behaviors in Three Outdoor Contexts.* This study explored the differences found in children's play on the playground before and after changes were made and also examined if play in the meadow shifted due to the new more nature-oriented playscape at the school. In addition, these researchers examined if the final design of the new outdoor space matched the teachers' and children's expectations. The lead pre-kindergarten teacher who headed up this project was also a doctoral student. Her team consisted of a part-time administrator, who was in the dissertator phase of her work, as well as two lead teachers.

One of the lead toddler teachers led a third research group that was supported by the studio teacher, a student teacher liaison, and the school Director. This project entitled, *Toddler Responses to the Campus Landscape* focused on one toddler class's explorations of the physical spaces on and around the Kent State University Campus. The primary data gathering method used in this project was videotaping of the children on their trips around campus. Research team members analyzed and interpreted how the children responded to their explorations of both natural and physical landscapes.

The final research group project led by one lead pre-kindergarten teacher and supported by two lead teachers and the Director was entitled, *How Children Communicate through Materials.* Focusing on the Reggio Emilia-inspired notion that children express themselves through all different types of materials (Edwards, Gandini, & Forman, 2011), this group studied the evolution of the artwork of two focal children who spoke English as a second language. The aim of this research was to explore how children communicated through a variety of art materials (clay, paint, crayons, etc.).

Time was provided for each research team to work together during weekly one-and-a-half-hour faculty meetings. Teams worked on data gathering and data analysis, and portions of the literature review were collaboratively written during these weekly meetings. Collaborative work stemming from three of the four research projects was shared at a local Visitation Day and conference that was held at the Child Development Center as well as at the international Reconceptualizing Early Childhood Education (RECE) conference that was held at Kent State

University in 2014. As a consequence of sharing their work during the Visitation Day, CDC teachers have been invited by other centers to present workshops and share their insights with other early childhood professionals. Clearly, much time and energy have gone into the research being conducted by the teachers. Moving the projects toward the publication phase has been difficult.

Three of the projects have resulted in written work that has been submitted for publication. One of the projects that moved along rather quickly was the one that was led by the pre-kindergarten teacher who is also doing doctoral work. This makes sense as she has been writing up portions of this work for credit in one of her doctoral courses. This added level of accountability was definitely a motivator to get the study completed. In addition, as mentioned above, one of her team members was also a dissertator who has a deep understanding of the research process and writing for publication. While the time and space provided for the research projects concluded at the end of the school year, these two team members continued to meet and write together throughout the summer months and into the new school year. Thus, this continued in some ways, the historical RE-inspired approach/documentation while allowing it to generate into a full-fledged sharable research study. Yet, the expectations for conducting and writing-up research at the center had shifted. First, through formalizing the research process in ways such as requiring that all teachers complete the Collaborative Institutional Training Initiative (CITI program) and adding teacher input to the Institutional Review Board paperwork, research outcomes were taken more seriously. Research also became a higher priority in the daily lives of teachers. For example, conducting research, and making presentations and authoring publications at least once every three years, were skills that were included in the annual teacher assessment tool in 2013 that was created by a small group of teachers and gained consensus from the entire faculty.

The biggest challenges to completing the research projects are the lack of time, financial remuneration, and teacher knowledge and confidence in research/writing skills. The classroom teachers at the CDC are scheduled to work eight-hour days, yet each one puts in hours that extend well beyond their compensated work time. The Director was able to offer some additional compensation for writing in the summer as the teachers do follow an academic schedule, and three people contemplated this idea. Yet, each of the three teachers found it difficult to find the time and space to write during days and nights that are already packed full with professional and personal responsibilities. Moving into the second year of the goal of making the research public, one teacher proposed release time during the academic year to write two afternoons a week. She was able to leave the classroom and focus on writing for the period of time she was out of the classroom. An article was submitted and is in review at the time of this writing. Finally, among this particular group of teachers, there is a lack of confidence and education about research and writing with a research focus versus writing for a practitioner audience. While faculty meeting sessions that focused on research topics such as crafting a literature review, data analysis, and the writing process, were organized, it is difficult to apply and sustain this type of emerging work when you are also fully immersed in teaching children, mentoring pre-service teachers, and meeting state "star award" standards.

We are in the process of contemplating ways that the actual write-up of the research could be more fully supported. One way early childhood faculty are working to support the write-up of research of the laboratory school is through the creation of a graduate writing seminar entitled, *Writing for Publication in Early Childhood*. The first time the seminar was offered (spring 2015), the CDC teachers were too busy to take it, but one doctoral student who had taught at the CDC was able to move some of her teacher action research toward publication. This course was designed by Lash (first author) to provide support to take a writing project through to publication. A second way to support writing for publication would be to pair Center teachers with early childhood faculty who could guide them in an Independent Study format. In contrast to lab schools that use full-time graduate assistants as teachers, this suggestion allows for the structure that the teachers need to bring this work to fruition as contrasted with a graduate student as lab school teacher who might use these findings for university course-work. This format would provide support and accountability as they write up the research, with the added benefit of providing them with needed continuing credits toward our state "star award." Finally, there has been discussion about how we could restructure the school day for teachers who are willing to spend some of their paid time writing for publication. Teachers will be asked to write a proposal specifying the writing project on which they will work and the amount of time they feel they would need to complete that process. There would be an account-ability system put in place with the Director whereby teachers would need to check in to share their progress. For example, a teacher would need to meet with the Director three to four times per semester to discuss the progress that is being made on the research project and share how the work will be moved into the public sphere. This would allow the CDC teachers productive processes for criti-cal reflection on the intersection of theory and practice in their own classrooms (Cochran-Smith & Lytle, 1990) resulting in information that would be dissemi-nated beyond the center.

Exploratory Model Two: Participatory Action Research Approach

Participatory action research is a collaborative approach to conducting research that is undertaken by a group of people who intend to have their work result in some action, change, or improvement on the issue under study (Kindon, Pain, & Kesby, 2007). Participatory action research differs from the CDC Team Approach in that the final goal is the improvement of something (curriculum, assessment, administration) within the school context. We embarked upon the research knowing that we would be shifting the curriculum in one of the classrooms as a result of our study. The research team consisted of a lead teacher and her associate teacher, a graduate student, and the Director. We engaged in this research because we wanted to make certain that each child had the opportunity to shape a positive social identity within the "formal" curriculum that was offered in the early childhood classroom. The research question was: "How can we make visible the home and community resources that young children bring with them to school in order to create a more inclusive preschool curriculum?" The research team was prepared to take action to shift the curriculum based on the data we gathered from the children. This research holds many of the ADS tenets. Particular relevance is for the first part of the definition, which focuses on the three conjoint emphases of Applied, Developmental, and Science. This section highlights the *Applied* emphases due to "direct implications for what individuals, families, practitioners, and policymakers do" (Lerner, Wertlieb, & Jacobs, 2005, p. 6). The next section highlights the *Developmental* emphases as the research team looks at change over time; finally, we can easily identify varied and robust research methods that ground this approach in *Science* (Lerner et al., 2005).

The study was comprised of three phases. During Phase I, the Director, who was the lead researcher, and a graduate student observed the classroom of 21 children, ages 3–5 from culturally, linguistically, and economically diverse backgrounds over a period of three months. The research team met weekly to discuss how children were responding to the "formally" planned preschool curriculum and worked to identify those who were not as engaged in the curriculum as their peers. Throughout the research study, the graduate student and university researcher were reading various scholarly articles and, when appropriate to the project, shared aspects of these readings with the lead and associate teacher.

At the start of Phase 2, we asked each child in the class to take 20 to 25 digital photographs of "*things you do when you are not at school*" in order to make visible the funds of knowledge (González, Moll, & Amanti, 2005) children brought with them from home into school. While each child had an opportunity to share three to five of their photographs with the entire class, the four focal children were invited to meet with pairs of co-investigators to participate in photo-elicitation interviews (Rose, 2012). During the photo-elicitation interviews the children, accompanied by their parents/guardians, were asked to share any or all of the 25 images they captured with their digital cameras. Once all of the focal children had an opportunity to share their images, the co-investigators conducted a content analysis of the photo-elicitation interviews and worked collaboratively to create curriculum incorporating the codes and themes embedded in the funds of knowledge (González, Moll, & Amanti, 2005) that were made visible through the content analysis.

During Phase 3, research team members worked together to shape curriculum that incorporated the themes that emerged from the photo-elicitation interviews and conducted another series of observations to gather data on how children responded to the shifts that were made in the curriculum.

Although the lead classroom teacher read each draft of the paper and added information to the sections that we designated for her to write, the university researcher and graduate student took the lead in writing up the research for publication. Unfortunately, the associate teacher was not as involved in the data analysis or writing up the research for publication as we thought he might be. However, he did provide verbal input when asked. The Director, classroom teacher, and graduate student presented this research at the international RECE conference held at Kent State University in the fall of 2014 and an article was submitted to a Tier I research journal. This research was replicated and a second prekindergarten classroom was added. The classroom teacher who joined the project became a part of the research team. Collaborative articles are being written for publication on the methodological aspects of this replicated study as well as on the curriculum development. The lead researcher presented the research methodology at the European Research Network about Parents in Education (ERNAPE) annual conference on behalf of the team, and a conference proposal, which was authored by all current research team members, was accepted to the annual meeting of the American Education Research Association (AERA). Prior to 2012, research was focused at the practitioner level, not presented, discussed, and critiqued among other researchers at national or international research conferences such as AERA, RECE, and ERNAPE. We are working toward a more balanced approach, as we acknowledge the value of multiple types of educational research.

Exploratory Model Three: Summer STEAM Camp Approach

A third research model that has been introduced at the Child Development Center consists of a group of University faculty who taught alongside a CDC faculty member during a 10-week summer STEAM (Science, Technology, Engineering, Art, & Mathematics) camp program. STEAM camp served children from 3 to 6 years of age from 9:00a.m. to 12:00 noon. Ten week-long sessions with titles such as, *Science and Me*, *Engineers in Training*, and *Wonders of Water* were offered during the camp. A CDC faculty member facilitated all of the sessions and science education faculty and graduate assistants provided information and taught lessons on their area of interest. They were also invited to conduct research during the time they spent at the Center. For example, one University researcher and her graduate students presented a series of camp sessions on different science topics. In each session children were immersed in discussions about science and scientists. During the first session, the children were asked to define what the word "scientist" meant to them. In subsequent sessions the science experts/researchers referred to scientists and the scientific process. At the end of the ten weeks, the children were again asked to describe the job of a scientist. Currently, these researchers are in the process of writing up the data they gathered.

During the summer STEAM camp of 2014, four STEAM-related proposals were submitted and approved by the Kent State University Institutional Review Board. To date, one article, "Dig into fossils!" (Borgerding, 2015) has been published and one article, "Understanding the Body: A Series of Activities Designed to Teach PreK Children about Human Anatomy" (Raven, in press) has been accepted for publication, both in *Science and Children*. Other articles are either in process or in review. This model takes the burden of data analysis and writing from the CDC teachers and places the responsibility on university researchers who benefit greatly from the opportunity to conduct research at the laboratory school. While the CDC may be referenced in these articles, the teachers are not listed as authors of the publications as their role is teaching and it is not at the center of the research being conducted. They were not involved in writing or reviewing the work.

This model has its challenges, as science education faculty do not necessarily have an understanding of the best practices of teaching young children nor do they always choose data collection methods that work best in an early childhood setting. While there is definitely a healthy respect between and among university personnel and CDC faculty and staff, this is the research model that seems to take the most time to negotiate. Yet, we believe it may be the most important. First, we are working with and learning from science faculty who are doing cutting-edge work in their fields. It keeps us abreast of innovations and shifting trends in science education. Second, hosting researchers from various departments across the university positions the laboratory school as belonging to the university community. Cutting funding or outsourcing a university asset becomes much more difficult when there are researchers across campus invested in the laboratory school as a place for exemplary teaching as well as a research center.

Reflections on the Shifts in Practice

Deciding to expand the CDC research paradigm beyond self-study to a more systematized, public research paradigm has created possibilities for the CDC to truly be part of a lab school consortium that adheres to an ADS model. This expansion still allows for the study of the day-to-day life in lab schools as well as acknowledging the science requirement to make this knowledge generation public and allows for the reciprocal relationship between application and science. This points to greater impact for the CDC; visibility and making the teachers' and faculty's hard work public; robust and varied research methodologies; as well as larger, more diverse populations with whom to study and collaborate. Clearly the rigor and self-discipline that the teachers have shown with self-examination, reflective thinking, internal documentation, and accountability, have been transferred and readily applied to wider application and dissemination through the exploratory research models under way by the CDC. As evidenced by the review of Table 3.1 clear gains in making the work public have been made since August of 2012. While solid, inspirational, credible inquiry work was occurring at the CDC, the current leadership's deliberate efforts for research and follow-through in national and international presentations and publications have shown significant gains. The table also contains a column delineating whether or not the research study would align in a lab school consortium model utilizing an applied developmental science model; gains toward this stance are evident also. Reflection on these accomplishments at the CDC has also broadened ideas for qualitative and quantitative methodological research at the Center.

In retrospect, we can relate to South Dakota State University's reflective commentary (Cutler et al., 2009) as they describe their lab school and teacher education program's journey to build a culture of teacher research. While their definition focused more on reflective teaching practices and engagement with teaching as an inquiry activity, the CDC similarly strived to create a culture of research that built upon the teacher action research that was strongly in place and to move that "inquiry"—with internal documentation—to external research for the broader early childhood community to access. During SDSU's change process, they identified a trend of "valuing outside perspectives" that is resonating with our CDC journey, and "the need to move beyond the comforts and familiarity of our own experiences and to incorporate and learn from multiple perspectives" (Cutler et al., 2009, p. 413).

It is important to articulate the efforts the CDC teachers and leaders have made to stay balanced in their lab school's tri-part mission, to attend to the care and education of children in the program as the highest priority while continuing pre-service teacher development and striving for increased research (McMullen & Lash, 2012). Similar to what Cutler et al. (2009) determined, reflection shows we have moved from the question of *why* we should make a shift in our culture of research to *how* to make this shift while meeting all parts of the mission.

As we have shifted our culture of research, we understand that this has provided a robust professional development experience for our teachers and ourselves (Roberts, Crawford, & Hickman, 2010). We have changed the way we "close the circle" of inquiry. In fact, now we close the inquiry circle by taking the final step and make our research public. In this way, we meet thresholds that would be better aligned for the consortium ADS model. We also believe we will embed our new learning into systematic practice as part of the culture of research and this will bring benefit to our teachers and pre-service teachers at the CDC (Castle, 2013).

Thus, expanding the CDC research paradigm beyond self-study is having greater impact. In view of the digital and informational revolution for all learners/teachers, advances in the KSU Early Childhood Pre-service Teacher Education program to focus on global interconnectedness, the CDC's established RE-inspired approach, the CDC's recent expansion of its outdoor learning laboratory, an increase in more CDC student and international families, an increased interest

TABLE 3.1 KSU CDC Research Efforts & Models from 2007–2016

Research Efforts (2007–2012)	Teachers and Researchers	Culminating Experience	Research Made Public	Research Consortium w/ADS Model Potential?
Self-Study Experiences				
Study Group with South Dakota State University	Program Teachers and University faculty; both sites	Teacher exchange visits; interactive distance video book study groups	One refereed journal article; one book chapter; one national presentation	Yes
Prairie Partners	Leadership Team and Faculty from each site	Observation tool piloted for several semesters at KSU; feedback was shared with consortium	No	Not in current format
Reggio Emilia inspired projects for each class for the semester/year	One kindergarten, two toddler, and four preschool classrooms	End of School Year Celebration of Learning festival with documentation in classrooms and school hallways—(internal)	No	Not in current format
Collaborative community relationships with master gardeners, fraternities, national park personnel	Ongoing and thriving community partnerships are key to the inquiry practices of each classroom	Field trips, community speakers/groups visiting the center, to facilitate children's research/understanding	No	Not in current format

Exploratory Models (August 2012 to present)	Teachers and Researchers	Culminating Experience	Research Made Public	Research Consortium w/ADS Model Potential?
CDC Team Approach	4 teams/4 members/1 team leader	Shared work during CDC Visitation Day and Conference (2013)	One publication under review and one in process; three local presentations; three international presentations	Yes
Participatory Action Research Approach	4 co-investigators—university researcher, lead teacher, associate teacher/graduate assistant/graduate student/ independent study	Shared work during CDC Visitation Day Tours (2014)	Two international presentations; one journal article under peer review; one journal article in process; one replication of study in another classroom at lab school	Yes
Summer STEAM Camp Approach	Science and math teacher education professors and their graduate students; consider how to involve technology and arts faculty	Children benefit from expert teachers in both early childhood and in science and math; cross pollination for the teachers and researchers	One journal article published; one journal article in press; additional articles in process	Yes

in family engagement, and a transition in leadership to a research orientation, we can identify numerous positive indicators to consider research opportunities with an ADS model. Considering the rigor and self-discipline that the teachers have shown with self-examination, reflective thinking, internal documentation, and accountability, the reality of gently reorganizing efforts gives realistic plans and hope for wider application and dissemination. This is clear in the work of the past three years with three robust exploratory models of research, all of which move beyond self-study and two of which have already reached the research threshold of making the work public through publications. Scholarly significance is gained from increasing the range of research to look outward and look to dissemination of the lab school's diligent work in addition to the CDC's historical stance of self-study. These efforts would complement an alignment with the ADS consortium.

References

Borgerding, L. A. (2015). Dig into fossils! *Science and Children, 52*(9), 30–37.

Castle, K. (2013). The state of teacher research in early childhood teacher education. *Journal of Early Childhood Teacher Education, 34*(3), 268–286.

Cochran-Smith, M., & Lytle, S. L. (1990). Teacher research and research: The issues that divide. *Educational Researcher, 19*(2), 2–11.

Cutler, K., Bersani, C., Hutchins, P., Bowne, M., Lash, M., Kroeger, J., Brokmeier, S., Venhuizien, L., & Black, F. (2012). Laboratory schools as places of inquiry: A collaborative journey for two laboratory schools. *Early Education and Development, 23*(2), 242–258.

Cutler, K., Gilkerson, D., Bowne, M., & Stremmel, A. (2009). Change within a teacher education program and laboratory: A reflective commentary. *Journal of Early Childhood Teacher Education, 30*, 404–417.

Edwards, C., Gandini, L., & Forman, G. (Eds.). (2011). *The hundred languages of children: The Reggio Emilia experience in transformation.* ABC-CLIO.

Elicker, J., & Barbour, N. (2012) (Guest Eds.). Introduction to the special issues on university laboratory preschools in the 21st century. *Early Education and Development,* 139–142.

File, N. (2012). Identifying and addressing challenges to research in university laboratory preschools. *Early Education and Development, 23*(2), 143–152.

González, N., Moll, L. C., & Amanti, C. (Eds). (2005). *Funds of knowledge: Theorizing practices in households, communities and classrooms.* Mahwah, NJ: L. Erlbaum Associates.

Kindon, S., Pain, R., & Kesby, M. (2007). *Participatory action research approaches and methods: Connecting people, participation and place.* New York: Routledge.

Lerner, R. M., Wertlieb, D., & Jacobs, F. (2005). Historical and theoretical bases of Applied Developmental Science. In R. M. Lerner, F. Jacobs, & D. Wertlieb (Eds.), *Applied Developmental Science: An advanced textbook* (pp. 1–29). Thousand Oaks, CA: Sage.

McBride, B. A., Groves, M., Barbour, N., Horm, D., Stremmel, A., Lash, M., Bersani, C., Ratekin, C., Moran, J., Elicker, J., & Toussaint, S. (2012). Child Development Laboratory schools as generators of knowledge in early childhood education: New models and approaches. *Early Education and Development, 23*(2), 153–164.

McMullen, M. B., & Lash, M. (Fall 2012). Babies on campus: Service to infants and families among competing priorities in university child care programs. *Early Childhood Research and Practice, 14*(2).

Raven, S. (in press). Understanding the body: A series of activities to teach preK children about human anatomy. *Science and Children*.

Roberts, S. K., Crawford, P. A., & Hickman, R. (2010). Teacher research as a robust and reflective path to professional development. *Journal of Early Childhood Teacher Education, 31*(3), 258–271.

Rose, G. (2012). *Visual methodologies: An introduction to researching with visual materials.* Open University, UK: Sage Publications.

4

RESEARCHER–TEACHER COLLABORATIONS IN APPLIED RESEARCH IN A UNIVERSITY LABORATORY SCHOOL

Elizabeth Schlesinger-Devlin, James Elicker, and Treshawn Anderson

The goals and missions of most university-based child development laboratory schools (hereafter referred to as UBCD lab schools) are to serve as 1) a professional training site for future early childhood professionals; 2) a nucleus for various types of child development or early care and education research; and 3) a model of high quality early care and an education program for the community (Osborn, 1991), all while providing a safe, developmentally appropriate learning environment for young children and a supportive service for their families. Considering the amount of research and professional preparation that occurs in many UBCD lab schools, adopting an applied developmental science (ADS) perspective to guide the mission to engage in research can help to ensure the lab school is maximizing its potential to be a valuable resource for the university and the wider field of early education and care (Lerner et al., 2005; McBride et al., 2012). The first guiding principle of this ADS approach is that real-world problems of children, families, and professionals provide a focus for rigorous scientific inquiry (Lerner et al., 2005). ADS-focused researchers can use the context of the UBCD lab school to understand and explore how theoretical principles or new approaches to practice are "enacted in the natural laboratory of the real world" (Lerner et al., 2005, p. 9). A second guiding principle of ADS is that there are complementary and reciprocal relations between practice and research. "ADS work is reciprocal: science drives application, and application drives science" (Lerner et al., 2005, p. 7). For example, teaching practices within lab schools are often derived from child development theory and research (i.e. science drives application), but also the rigorous evaluation of these teaching practices in a lab school context can drive further development of theory and research, i.e. application drives science (Lerner et al., 2005). UBCD lab schools provide an ideal context for reciprocal collaborations among early childhood educators and researchers. This productive

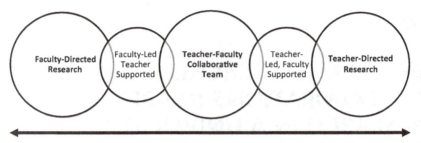

FIGURE 4.1 Continuum of Collaborative Relationships between Lab School Teachers and Faculty Researchers.

reciprocity in research participation can be actualized in a variety of ways. Some of the possibilities are illustrated by using a collaboration continuum, ranging from faculty-directed research to teacher-directed research, with faculty-teacher collaborations of various kinds in the center (see Figure 4.1).

The collaboration framework outlined and illustrated in this chapter helps to illustrate a variety of examples of the ADS approach as actualized in lab schools, using a continuum model that includes varying levels of involvement and engagement by both faculty researchers and laboratory school teachers. As shown in Figure 4.1, at one end of the spectrum is lab school teacher-directed research, sometimes known as participatory or teacher-action research (Mertens, 2010), in which lab school teachers are in primary control of the conceptualizing and planning of a research project, the execution of the project or program, and interpretation and use of the research findings. At the other end of the spectrum is faculty-led research, which includes limited participation from the classroom educators in the planning, execution, and interpretation of the research. Lab school teachers may assist in the selection of participants in the research or may carry out experimental procedures under the direction of the faculty researcher. They may have helpful observations or other kinds of input for the faculty researcher, but they are not in a directive role. In between these ends of the spectrum are varying degrees of collaborative balance. This continuum is not a rigid description of participation or interactions within research, rather a heuristic for describing variations and degrees of collaboration. Some research processes are dynamic. A study may begin in the faculty-directed research mode, move to a collaborative mode in the middle of the process, and then back to a more faculty-directed mode in the data analysis and interpretation phase of the project. At the center of the continuum are various forms of truly collaborative research, in which faculty and lab school teachers work together as equal partners to develop the goals, objectives, and approach of a research project that is mutually beneficial for all members of the research group.

Bennett, Gadlin, and Levine-Finley (2010) use a continuum in discussing working as a team to conduct research. Implementing applied developmental research involves a range of relationships, tasks, and responsibilities. This chapter shares examples of collaborative relationships of researchers and lab school teachers along this continuum, within the early childhood lab school setting. The examples depict successful research collaborations that involve a variety of combinations of expert input, control, and direction from early childhood professionals and academic research faculty. While the labels in Figure 4.1 indicate three main categories of collaborative research, in fact there are many possible combinations of control, collaboration, and support when the research process is considered in all its aspects, over time, in the conduct of a project. Therefore the continuum should be considered a heuristic device or starting point for understanding various kinds of potential research collaboration within UBCD lab schools.

The Ben & Maxine Miller Child Development Laboratory School (MCDLS) is a university-based early childhood program for children birth to age five, housed in the Human Development and Family Studies department at Purdue University. The staff, children, and parents at MCDLS engage in various kinds of research collaborations, both within their home department and with faculty researchers from other departments within the university. The program mission of MCDLS is to be a "loving community of discovery" including children, teachers, parents, university students, and researchers, so collaborative research fits nicely with this mission. Lab schools like MCDLS are in a unique and advantageous position to foster collaboration among various stakeholders when it comes to engaging in research. Embracing the role of informed intermediaries, lab school educators can help families and researchers come to mutual understandings about the importance of research that is conducted to produce new knowledge about the real-world problems of children, families, and teachers. A unique benefit offered by lab schools is that research is "front and center" in the mission of the organization, and families understand this as they consider the program for their child. In many lab schools, a time-tested research protocol has been established, including guidelines for appropriate research and review of research proposals by the staff, sometimes with assistance by faculty advisers. The lab school setting therefore offers a well-established site for research, often as a central part of its mission, and promotes understanding and acceptance by all involved: teachers, children, families, administrators, and faculty researchers (Wilcox-Herzog & McLaren, 2012). Teachers at the lab school have structured time in their schedules that allows for their participation in research. The Miller lab school facility also offers unique benefits for researchers in that there are spacious classrooms that allow observers to work without interfering with ongoing activities, smaller testing rooms within the center, and observation booths with one-way mirrors and amplified sound attached to every early childhood classroom. Lab schools, with their unique focus on research, as well as early education, care, and family support, can serve as incubators for applied research that fosters new ideas, new knowledge, and new professional practices. Research and research-based practices developed collaboratively within the lab school can be shared on a larger scale with community-based early childhood programs that do not have the opportunity or the resources to do their own research on-site. The fact that lab school research is done in a relatively "real-world setting" rather than in an artificial laboratory, and that researchers are respectfully collaborating with early educators in research and practice, makes lab schools a prime site for realizing the goals of applied developmental science (ADS.) Using the ADS research faculty–teacher collaboration continuum presented here as a framework, this chapter will present examples of productive ADS-collaborations that have occurred in university lab schools around the country, including in the Purdue University MCDLS.

Faculty-Directed Research

On one end of the collaborative relationships continuum is faculty-directed research. Faculty-directed research involves little or no collaboration between the faculty and teachers. The faculty researcher is focused on a specific goal for research and is conducting that research with participants within the lab school. The participants typically are the children of parents enrolled in the laboratory school, and the research is not focused on the teaching staff. Examples of faculty-led research in a lab school setting include measurement development, fidelity training, research method course assignments, and other projects in which laboratory school teachers do not have a strong collaborative role. Lab schools can create a pool of subjects available for researchers. The research subjects may be recruited conveniently when families and/or teachers are available as part of the target population for a researcher.

One example of faculty-led research is illustrated by a study conducted to train researchers on using specific measures and data collection methodology. For example, MCDLS was involved in a research project entitled, "The longitudinal relation between early mathematical and non-mathematical skills" (Purpura & Napoli, 2015). In this study the faculty researcher began with a need to train graduate and undergraduate students on the measures used to collect data about early mathematics learning with young children. These researchers would later conduct research with a larger sample in the surrounding community. Children in the laboratory school were individually assessed by a student researcher while the faculty researcher guided and offered feedback. In this case there was little formal interaction between the faculty researcher and the laboratory school teachers. The conveniently located and cooperative lab school setting made it relatively easy for the faculty researcher to train the data collectors in preparation for the larger study.

Another example of faculty-led research was the development of an observation tool designed to assess children's motor skills, social engagement, and early engineering behaviors (Gold et al., in press). Researchers observed children in various play areas within the laboratory school to document the frequency of these behaviors in efforts to determine which behaviors would be necessary to include in the final measure. Once the measure was completed, the researchers conducted reliability observations prior to utilizing the measure, both within the lab school and out in the community.

Another study that demonstrates faculty-directed research focused on the topic of hunger in young children (Brauchla, 2013). Nutrition science researchers collected data indicating if a child was hungry or full. In this study the researcher read a story to the children before snack time. The researcher created a story which described and defined the concept of hungry and full through illustrations and text. Upon completion of the story, the researcher asked each child if they were hungry or full. The researcher recorded the children's answers and then left the classroom and went into the observation booth to observe the children. The classroom teacher announced the opportunity for the children to have their snack. The researcher noted which children ate their snack and which children did not eat their snack. The information was coded to determine if the children who had stated they were hungry or full earlier, ate their snack when it was provided, or refrained from eating their snack. This research study was primarily conducted at the faculty researchers' direction. While the lab school teachers participated by making time for the story and following the snack necessary procedures, they contributed little else to this research.

Faculty-Led/Teacher-Supported Research

Another kind of research engagement within faculty-directed research is faculty-led/teacher-supported research. The faculty has a directive role in this type of research collaboration by conducting the overall planning and implementation of the research project, and the teacher is a participant, while lending a greater degree of information and support than in the previous examples. This aspect of the collaborative continuum includes research in which the lab school teachers are the subjects of research, contributing data in various ways.

An example of faculty-led/teacher-supported research concerns faculty who are looking to fine-tune their research questions. In one study, the researcher asked teachers to express their beliefs about math and mathematical concepts in early childhood teaching (Richardson & Bofferding, 2015). The teachers responded to 20 questions the researcher posed in a pilot study. This input from the lab school teachers then aided in evaluating and refining the terminology and conceptual clarity of the questions. The refined questions were used in subsequent studies conducted with a larger sample of early childhood teachers. In this project the researcher also observed the classroom teachers implementing math activities with the children in the lab school. The researcher asked the teachers to direct their focus on math skills specific to the questions included in the survey when they implemented their lesson. The lab school teachers' early input was a valuable example of faculty-led/teacher-supported research. This collaboration early in the research process resulted in more realistic and practical perspectives about the teachers' knowledge, understanding, and ways of communicating about math in an early childhood setting. The findings of this research project will help guide professional development training and best practices in mathematical instruction in the early childhood classroom. A benefit of working with lab school teachers for this research was the availability of the teachers and the quick response time. Teachers in the lab school have daily planning periods, access to computers, and office space, all of which facilitated their contributions to the measures developed in the research project. Also the typical higher levels of teacher experience and education, plus the focus of research in the mission of the lab school, make the lab school teachers ideal subjects for this kind of collaborative research, as compared to community-based early educators, who often have less time and experience and are more focused on providing a service to children and families.

Another example of faculty-led/teacher-supported research involved the development of a curriculum beliefs and intentions scale, intended for use in the lab school and other early care and education settings, once refined and validated. A graduate student and faculty researcher initially developed a measure describing infant/toddler teacher beliefs about developmentally appropriate education and care. Prior to mass distribution for a psychometric study of this new scale, the researchers piloted the measure with a select group of infant/toddler professionals, including the lab school teachers. Lab school teachers were not only asked to complete the measure, but also to provide specific feedback on the scale items, including their relevance, clarity, and importance (DeVellis, 2003).

The items in the measure included beliefs about typical everyday practices of infant/toddler teachers, beliefs about responding to infant crying, separating mobile from non-mobile infants, and formally introducing academic concepts to children in the infant/toddler classroom. Since most faculty researchers do not have direct daily contact with teachers and toddlers in the early care and educational setting, it was critical to have experienced lab school teachers' opinions about the relevance and importance of the scale items to determine if items had adequate face validity and should remain in scale or be eliminated. Good scale items are characterized by the use of clear terminology (DeVellis, 2003). Lab school teachers, who are familiar with research, have worked with novice teachers-in-training, and who are aware of typical contemporary early care and education issues and terminology, can assist in making items in a measure clear to novice or inexperienced infant/toddler teachers who will be completing the scale in the future. In the early stages of measures development, it is especially helpful to have input from well-educated, experienced early educators such as those found in the lab school.

Upon completion of the pilot study, the researchers evaluated the lab school teachers' feedback and adjusted the measure accordingly. Although lab school teachers assisted in providing feedback on the measure, the goals, content, and procedures of the research remained under the control of the faculty researchers. The researchers took into consideration the feedback from lab school teacher respondents; however, decisions to make final adjustments were made by the researchers. This is an example of a faculty-led, teacher-supported collaboration, because the researchers had a directive role, and lab school teachers participated and provided supportive input.

A final example of faculty-led, teacher-supported research can be seen in an MCDLS project that involved research by a mechanical engineering faculty and undergraduate students. The project began with a faculty-driven expectation for their undergraduate class, but evolved early in the process from faculty leadership to significant teacher participation and leadership. Students in the mechanical engineering class were charged with creating a baby product that would solve a problem or address a need in infant child care. Lab school teachers met with the students to talk about the products they currently use in the classroom. Lab school teacher and mechanical engineering students brainstormed various projects which the students could develop. The lab school teachers' expertise informed and guided the students' proposed ideas. Following this brainstorming, the students made classroom observations, guided by lab school teachers, in which they collected data on the types of behaviors they observed with infants and toddlers; capabilities of the infants and toddlers; equipment most often used by infants; and observations of different colors and textures used in the infant classroom. The lab school teachers then held follow-up sessions with the students in which they shared their observations about needs in the infant/toddler classrooms. These follow-up sessions also included additional brainstorming and suggestions of ideas by the lab school teachers. The student teams then worked together to create a product. The students built a product prototype and brought it back to the classroom for testing. Together with the lab school teachers, the engineering students and their faculty instructor evaluated the success or limitations of the prototype products. This sequence of product development and evaluation was ongoing, including approximately three cycles of prototype and product testing.

This teacher-student collaboration, under the supervision of a faculty course instructor, creating a product to assist in the care of infants, is an example of an ADS approach in research and teaching within the lab school. The students' learning process, initiated by the faculty instructor, guided by lab school teachers, informed the design process of the students creating products that could address particular needs within infant/toddler classrooms. Although this student research and design process was initiated by the faculty member, it was the active participation and leadership of the lab school teachers that guided the project to a successful conclusion.

All of these examples demonstrate faculty leadership and faculty-directed research with various kinds of support and participation from the lab classroom teachers. The teachers participated—however, there was little collaboration in the formulation of research questions or methods used. A benefit of these types of studies for the lab school teachers was the exposure to new research and engineering concepts and perspectives. Anecdotally, conversations among the lab school teachers, after answering the questions in the math interview study, led to continued exploration and opportunities for self-reflection about approaches to early math teaching and learning. The lab school teachers talked with one another about their philosophy of math and beliefs about teaching math to young children. These conversations led individual educators to share their strengths and weaknesses, and created a support system—relying on one another to share resources and creative ways to implement math in the classroom, based on concepts and goals introduced by the research faculty during this research process. In a lab school setting, the opportunity to actively participate in and support research offers teachers opportunities for growth and a deeper understanding of best practices in working with young children and their families. Teachers understand that their role in an early childhood classroom within a lab school includes participation and contributions to research, a role that is not typical in a lab school community early childhood program. The higher educational requirements typically required of lab school teachers, often at least a bachelor's degree in child development or early education, also complement working effectively with researchers within a university setting.

Teacher-Faculty Collaborative Research

Recent investigations at MCDLS illustrate research collaborations that were balanced between faculty researchers and lab school teachers in terms of leadership and participation. The first example is a study of preschool children's play with the Imagination Playground™: large, lightweight, high-density foam building blocks. This research was funded by the A.L. Mailman Foundation and organized by the KaBOOM! organization (www.kaboom.org) which promotes play opportunities for American children. The faculty researchers, the lab school director, lab school teachers, and KaBOOM! program staff collaborated to design and implement an observational study of the behaviors of preschool children as they played: 1) with Imagination Playground™ (IP) blocks; 2) on the traditional playground; and 3) in the dramatic play or "house" area indoors. The IP play materials, called "large, loose parts," have long been popular in early childhood education settings, but seldom been systematically studied in this form. Throughout the planning and implementation of this study, researchers, lab school teachers, and KaBOOM! play educators exchanged ideas and made decisions about important research questions, how best to observe and describe children's play in the three play contexts, and how to interpret the observational data that resulted. Based on these conversations, this research team decided to observe children's social, physical, and early engineering play behaviors in three indoor and outdoor play settings, including play with the Imagination Playground blocks. Graduate student research assistants in the team conducted extensive time-sampled observations of children's play, and lab school and Head Start teachers met with the researchers in focus groups during the three-month study to exchange observations and impressions, and to discuss their thoughts about what the children were doing and how their play was developing over time. Further discussions about the play observations with both lab school teachers and parents occurred when the research team presented final study results in several research, staff, and family meetings.

This project had benefits to the lab school teachers in that they were able to introduce an innovative new play material into the school, observe and reflect on children's play across play contexts, and think about ways of supporting and enriching play with the Imagination Playground blocks. For researchers, the teachers' input throughout the process was essential in formulating research questions, incorporating significant play behaviors into the observation instrument, and interpreting the observational data in accurate and potentially useful ways. While the input of both lab school and Head Start teachers was valuable, the lab school teachers had the times and research perspectives that made their observations and suggestions especially valuable. Therefore this collaborative research project was producing information that, from the ADS perspective, was both driven by and driving application—even prior to any publication of results. The project attracted requests for presentations to practitioner and advocacy groups and was highlighted on the KaBOOM! web-site and the online TV program "Inside Science." This research was summarized in a recently published article in the scientific journal, *Children, Youth, and Environments* (Gold et al., 2015).

A second example from MCDLS illustrates the potential for productive faculty–lab school teacher collaboration in a professional development research project. In this case the Laboratory School assisted with the development, piloting, and field-testing of a new teacher-training program, focused on increasing the quality of adult–child interactions in early childhood classrooms. Based on research in the Netherlands, the Caregiver Interaction Profile (CIP) (Helmerhorst, Riksen-Walraven, Vermeer, Fukkink, & Tavecchio, 2014) was introduced to lab school teachers, community child care teachers, and professional development "coaches" who were either research faculty or Purdue Extension Educators. This collaborative research team met to refine the CIP translation from Dutch to English, to clarify the key interaction concepts so that American teachers would find them understandable, and to develop procedures for coaching that would promote high quality teacher–child interactions in the participating teachers' classrooms. In a pilot field test of this training model, coaches and lab school teachers worked weekly with the six CIP teacher–child interaction dimensions over two months, with teachers self-assessing, setting goals, trying new interactions highlighted in discussions with their coaches, and evaluating their progress on a weekly basis. As the pilot project proceeded, both coaches and teachers discussed and evaluated the coaching/learning process. Teachers and coaches documented their experiences and progress in writing. The project culminated with an all-day meeting of teachers, coaches, and faculty researchers to review the benefits and challenges of the CIP training process and suggest future directions for its development and use. Plans for further development and validation of the CIP scales and PD program are underway, and next steps will include continued collaboration among lab school educators and faculty researchers. One piece of evidence that the project had lasting value and impact for the lab school was that one lead teacher who was a member of the collaborative team subsequently began using the CIP framework to orient and train new co-teachers within her classroom. Again, while this project included both lab school teachers and community-based early educators, the contributions of the lab school teachers were especially valuable. The significant experience and research focus of the lab school teachers led to a deeper involvement and commitment to incorporating this new way of assessing classroom interactions and incorporating this framework into ongoing practice within the lab school classroom.

These examples illustrate productive collaborative approaches to research in lab schools that include a balance of leadership and participation, using ADS principles as a guide. Through these projects research faculty and lab school teachers discussed and negotiated research objectives, methodology, and results interpretation, with a goal of producing useful results. These collaborative processes contributed to the ADS goal of doing "science (that) drives application, and (making sure that) application drives science" (Lerner et al., 2005).

The projects we described above were primarily faculty-led, but at the same time had a high degree of collaboration with lab school teachers throughout the research process. The lab school teachers perceived a high level of ownership, input, and benefit while participating in these projects, more than they might have had with a traditional "take the data and run" approach used by faculty researchers in many lab schools in the past. The potential to produce useful results and engage audiences outside of the lab school and the academic department was enhanced by a combination of strong practice and scientific orientations in the research process within these collaborative projects.

Qualitative classroom case studies involving faculty researchers and lab school teachers are another type of research that can offer productive collaborative research opportunities. One example conducted by Britsch (2015) in MCDLS was a case study focused on children's development of a second language while participating in the English immersion environment of the lab school, using both photography and ethnographic data collection methods. This year-long project then led to continued study in a second year, with an extension focusing on photography and language development in the context of the dramatic play center. Throughout this two-year project, the faculty researcher worked closely with the same team of teachers, meeting weekly to discuss research goals, findings, and practical issues such as scheduling observations around nap/rest time and meals. The faculty researcher was embedded in the classroom weekly to collect data, focused especially on observations of six children. A benefit to implementing this kind of research within the lab school setting was the ability to conduct time intensive research, ongoing collaboration with teachers, and reflection by both the faculty research and the early educators. Again, the lab school setting offered unique opportunities, because the typical community-based early childhood teacher would not have the built-in time to conduct an intensive collaborative study for such a length of time.

The first study explored the question, "How do second language learners acquire scientific knowledge and concepts through the use of photography?" (Britsch, 2015). This collaboration began with discussions between the faculty researcher and the preschool teaching team about which science activities to implement within the classroom. The planning included discussion of the vocabulary, key concepts, and methodology for both the science learning opportunities and the research goals. Children were assigned cameras and encouraged to take pictures throughout the study. The researcher interviewed each child individually after each session. The researcher and the children met for 32 sessions, typically once a week during the academic semester. All children participated in taking pictures; the individual children who were a part of the study were given cameras that were identified with a number so the images could be downloaded to view later in follow-up interviews between the child and researcher. The researcher used an individual testing room within the Lab School to talk with each child, to review the photographs taken by the child, and to ask a series of questions about them. The questions about some of the science experiences were specific, such as talking about things that dissolved, and children were reminded they could take pictures throughout the classroom science experience. Once a science lesson was completed, the child and the researcher talked about the pictures taken during that experience. The lab school teachers were instrumental in the planning and implementation of the study, creating for the children developmentally appropriate questions and experiences related to science.

The second-year study, conducted by the same faculty researcher and lab school teachers, grew out of the first year data and focused on the development of literacy through dramatic play. The lab school teachers and the researcher collaborated in developing a series of dramatic play themes for the classroom, including the grocery store, restaurants, a flower shop, and a construction site. This study also lasted one year, and the team met together weekly to discuss themes for the dramatic play and ways to enrich the literacy environment. The researcher set up a video camera in the classroom to capture the children's interactions in the dramatic play area. The lab school teachers supported and assisted with data collection in various ways. The lab school teachers engaged the children in their play, asking them open-ended questions like "tell me about your job" or "describe what you are doing," which facilitated the research objectives. The lab school teachers also participated in the planning and brainstorming period prior to implementation of the dramatic play settings in the classroom. As a collaborative team the researcher and the lab school teachers developed the research questions and created the environment in which to conduct the research. The lab school teachers offered their experience and expertise in designing and structuring the dramatic play area. This study began as a faculty-led research study but quickly evolved into a collaborative relationship between the researcher and the lab school teachers, each offering expertise. The researcher was an expert in second language development and the lab school teachers were experts in play-based curriculum design.

The collective work completed in these successive case studies benefited all participants. The children were encouraged to increase their self- and environmental awareness and express themselves through science explorations, photography, dramatic play, and by representing their thoughts and feelings using language while playing. The teachers developed deeper skills for planning and implementing a scientific study and effective literacy instruction in the context of dramatic play in their classrooms, and the researcher was able to further her investigations of processes in early childhood learning by systematically collecting, analyzing, and interpreting the qualitative data. This research program contributed to the lab teachers' professional development, because the faculty researcher not only guided teachers' interactions with children during the study, but also provided training for all the teachers in the lab school while sharing the results of this research.

Teacher-Led Faculty-Supported Research

On the teacher-led side of the ADS research collaboration continuum are various forms of research conceived and implemented by lab school teachers, including: teacher-action research, teacher-as-scholar, and interactive research. Teacher researchers can work alone, with other teachers, or with faculty researchers (Abdal-Haqq, 1995). In these kinds of collaborative research, teachers in the classroom have a more directive role in deciding about the concept or topic of research, at times with the supportive consultation of a faculty researcher. Research should not always be rigidly defined as faculty-led, teacher-led, or teacher–faculty collaborative, because combinations or changes in the degree of collaboration may occur, even within one research project. The boundaries among the points in the research collaboration continuum are not always clearly delineated. However, regardless of the particular mix and development of teacher and researcher work together, successful collaborations in research teams are characterized by some degree of "sharing leadership, responsibility, decision-making authority ..." (Bennett, Gadlin, & Levine-Finley, 2010).

One example of teacher-directed faculty-supported research was in the area of methodology. The lab school teachers at MCDLS were questioning the validity of assessment tools implemented in the classroom to assist in identifying children with autism. The lab school teachers reached out to a faculty expert in the field of autism. The faculty member met with the lab school teachers to discuss the questions and what assessment tools were available to assist in evaluating children believed to have developmental delays, possibly on the autism spectrum. After the faculty researcher met with the teachers, she led a professional development training session for the lab school teachers, which included sharing an assessment tool (M-Chat, 2009). Once the lab school teachers had a tool to use for assessment the teachers brainstormed a plan, including implementing the assessment tool individually with the children in their classroom. The goal was to give each teacher an opportunity to explore the assessment tool and then reconvene afterwards to share reflections and observations gathered. Based on the observations and discussions the lab school teachers created a plan of application. The teacher determined that the tool was specific to evaluating children on the autism spectrum, and not necessarily a tool appropriate to use on an ongoing basis, or with typically developing children. Ultimately the lab school teachers created a procedure to implement the use of the assessment with children in the classroom and with parents to aid in the identification of developmental delays. This is an example of applied teacher-led research with a goal to develop a measure appropriate for use in the classroom, supported and resourced by a faculty researcher.

Another example of teacher-led faculty-supported research occurred in Brown, Googe, McIver, and Rathel's (2009) study of teacher-led physical activity interventions. The researchers wanted to study the effects of teacher-led physical activities on children's moderate to vigorous physical activity on the playground. The faculty researcher and lab school teacher worked together to develop two teacher-implemented physical activity interventions that would motivate children to increase or maintain their physical activity during outdoor play. After collaborative planning, the lab school teacher implemented intervention activities during the children's outdoor time, including holding discussions with the preschoolers about the importance of physical activity. The lab school teacher also selected focal students for trained observers to observe during his research project. Although the initial idea was sparked by the faculty researcher, the lab school teacher carried the responsibility for planning, designing, leading, and implementing the intervention in the classroom. The faculty researcher lent guidance in the development of a research question and advice about research design and methodology for a process that was primarily conceived and carried out by the lab school teacher.

Teacher-Directed Research

Teacher-directed research is characterized by the teacher's sole leadership in a project, which may or may not include fellow teachers, but includes little or no support from faculty researchers. This type of research may be informal or formal in its application, depending on the teacher's goal. In some cases, teacher-directed research is more formal and structured, such as when it entails accountability measurement for the classroom, assessment of program benchmarks or accreditation requirements, or creation of a program strategic plan. In other cases it may be less formal, such as when conducting developmental assessments on children, observing the interests and skills of children as a part of daily curriculum planning, or when introducing a new curriculum in the classroom. Teacher-directed research can also be focused on developing innovative experiences and activities or lessons for the children in the classroom.

A study by Scales, Perry, and Tracy (2012) at the Harold E. Jones Child Study Center at the University of California, Berkeley, provides an example of teacher-directed research. The classroom teachers evaluated the dynamics of the early childhood setting by systematically observing over time, reflecting, planning, and implementing aspects of their concepts of the "whole child." The teachers used an interpretative qualitative approach, which included:

- utilizing observations to determine how learning occurs through play in a developmentally appropriate classroom;
- enabling teachers to reflect on their beliefs, goals, and behavior and the influence of these on the context of the classroom;
- providing a basis for refinement and modification of the curriculum and environment that is based on direct observation;
- providing insights into how to intervene in an unobtrusive and relevant way and guide learning through self-directed play from the point of view of the children; and
- providing an authentic basis for evaluation and assessment of children and the environment (Scales et al., 2012, p. 166).

This interpretative approach guided the teachers to routinely observe the children within the classroom, and once they had made their observations the teachers met and reflected and shared their observations. The teaching team then created a plan of study based on the observations and discussions they had about the children. This plan was put into action through planned activities or experiences for the children. The observation–reflection–planning cycle commenced again once the activity or experience had been implemented in the classroom with the child. This study is an example of the teacher-led research within a classroom setting, where teachers planned the focus of their research and implemented their own data collection. The observations conducted by the teachers were aimed at developing a whole child approach in learning more about the children, describing the interests of the children, and noting relationships the children made with the environment, including peers and opportunities to employ various modes of learning. The observations and reflections were shared within the teacher research team (also known as the teaching team), which then enabled their planning for the next phase of the research, including the creation of experiences and activities to support the children's learning. New experiences and activities were then implemented in the classroom setting, and teachers continued their observations and assessments.

The Early Childhood Laboratory School at the University of California, Davis, also supports teachers to engage in teacher-directed research. For example, two lab school teachers in the preschool classrooms wanted to investigate how different early literacy environments affected children's language and literacy skill development. The classrooms took separate approaches to implementing an early literacy environment. Children's pre-literacy skills were then assessed at the end of the school year to determine which early literacy environment produced better literacy outcomes for children. This teacher-led research study informed the lab school teachers and other early childhood teachers about potential improvements to the literacy environment that can make a difference in children's pre-literacy skills (The Center for Child and Family Studies, 2015).

Another form of teacher-led research involves internal evaluations of program practice. The Ben and Maxine Miller Child Development Laboratory School maintains accreditation through the National Association for the Education of Young Children (NAEYC). As such, a yearly requirement for accreditation is conducting parent surveys. Questions on the parent surveys range from assessing the classroom environment, to program philosophy, to teacher engagement. The surveys are distributed, collected, and analyzed by the lab school teachers, and each classroom team is responsible for creating a strategic plan based on findings from the parent surveys. Each year these classroom strategic plans are evaluated and reviewed for growth and development by teachers and the lab school direc-tor. The benefits of the annual parent survey and evaluation of the strategic plans include the ability to address concerns expressed by parents and maintain areas of program strength. Reciprocal and supportive relationships between parents and teachers are important in working holistically toward each child's optimal devel-opment. Teachers' use of parent surveys to develop classroom strategic plans is an example of teacher-directed research in which the lab school teachers have sole leadership responsibilities.

A final example of a form of teacher-directed research is the sort of day-to-day inquiry practice that is typical of Reggio-inspired early childhood programs (Gandini, 2008) or of implementing the Project Approach (Helm & Katz, 2001). Teachers engage in research processes daily with the children by making obser-vations, posing research questions, collecting data, organizing and analyzing data, and drawing conclusions. Teachers plan opportunities for the children to engage in their own research. One example is collaboration with children to observe natural phenomena, such as the life cycles of butterflies. These types of teacher-directed research include children in the research process as co-investigators, uti-lizing their observations and documentation. Teachers and children are involved together in project-making or scientific study. Research methodology, the pro-cess of scientific inquiry, is thus shared with the children (i.e. hypothesizing what will happen next) as both teachers and children become co-constructors of knowledge.

The primary role of the early childhood classroom teacher in a full-day labo-ratory school like MCDLS is the daily care and education of the children, while keeping them safe and healthy, and helping them to meet their developmental goals. An additional characteristic of excellent early childhood teaching is using research to question, modify, and revisit teaching practices for continual profes-sional growth (Abdal-Haqq, 1995). Teachers who adopt a research perspective in their work, within their classroom team, within their center, or some degree of collaboration with professional researchers, are continually asking questions and updating their understanding about developmentally appropriate education, based on the results of their investigations. With the new discoveries and fresh understandings that come from collaboration in research, lab school teachers are able to implement current, innovative, research-based strategies to enhance child development.

Conclusions

The Applied Developmental Science (ADS) approach, viewed as a collaborative continuum and illustrated throughout this chapter, highlights real-life examples of research within a lab school setting. The conduct of research through collaborative relationships between faculty and lab school teachers, including sharing ideas, questions, leadership, and execution, provides a unique environment for conducting applied developmental and educational research. Lab schools have a mission to provide rich learning environments for young children and their families, but they are also settings for research. The receptive perspectives of the lab school teachers and families enrolled in the program work well with faculty eager to engage in problem-focused, real-world research. The continuum of collaborative relationships between lab school teachers and faculty researchers highlights many rich possibilities for productive applied research. Research collaborations of the sort we describe are appropriate to the mission and enriching for the lab school, which by definition is an environment of continual exploration and learning for young children. When teachers and other caring adults engage together in inquiry, this collaboration further enriches the experiences of both children and adults. Families feel a part of the process of learning more about and improving the quality of the early childhood program. The collaboration continuum offers a variety of options for research, depending on the particular mission, goals, resources, and other institutional supports and constraints that each lab school experiences. While the ideal collaborative research team might be viewed as one in which there is a perfect balance of shared leadership and responsibilities of the lab school teachers and faculty researchers, this type of shared collaboration may not always be suitable for some kinds of research, or in some lab school settings. However, some degree of teacher-researcher collaboration will often be productive in applied developmental research. Lab school programs can strive for new and helpful ways to develop the kinds of research collaboration we have discussed.

Emphasizing applied research within a laboratory school setting is not without constraints and limitations. Directors of early childhood lab schools benefit from having a well-rounded understanding for the support needed to conduct research within the lab school setting. The first challenge when research is encouraged may be an over-abundance of laboratory school research requests. There are multiple faculty researchers who submit applications to conduct research within MCDLS, potentially placing a strain on laboratory school administrators to objectively review numerous requests. Criteria for evaluating proposed research at MCDLS include: 1) assessing the number of projects being conducted at one time; 2) whether the research activities are developmentally appropriate and beneficial to the lab school program and the early childhood field; 3) and the amount of time and level of participation required of children and teachers. There is no simple answer to the question of how many studies are appropriate to have underway in the lab school at any one time. Often, the number of research projects approved for the lab school depends on the intensity of the research. An example of a low-impact research study was a project that was conducted over a short amount of time, seeking to evaluate children's retention of information using an iPad. This study was conducted within three, fifteen-minute sessions within one day. There-fore, the impact of the study on the daily classroom schedule was manageable (Han & Hollich, 2013). In contrast, some of the research examples provided above (e.g. children's science learning, photography, and literacy) were highly intensive for the children and teachers participating, and it was decided that it would be appropriate for only one study to be conducted within a classroom during that period. Likewise, teacher-directed research within one or more classrooms may be conducted at a level of involvement and intensity such that additional research studies are not possible within those rooms at that time.

Another potential limitation to conducting research in a lab school is gather-ing consent of multiple parties. Regardless of the program approval, parents always have the option to accept or decline their child's participation in any research study occurring within the lab school. In addition, once parents' consent for their child to participate in a study is established, the classroom teacher always has the prerogative to decline a research study or withdraw a child, based on the observed behavior of a child. Further, each child may also decline their participation in a study at any time in the research process. Although all approved studies follow the guidelines of the university's Human Subjects in Research Institutional Review Board (IRB) ethical standards, the requirements, and recommendations, obtain-ing teachers', parents', and children's consent to participate in research has often presented challenges.

The level of intrusiveness or disturbances to the preschool environment is another potential limitation to lab school research. Directors need to evaluate the research protocol. Is it developmentally appropriate for the target population? How disruptive will the research be for the participants in the study? Does the data collection methodology conflict with the requirements of outside regula-tory programs including state licensing requirements or accreditation guidelines? For example, one research study proposal focused on gathering children's stools to measure levels of proteins. This study was considered too invasive for the lab school environment, and the design protocols for collecting stools samples were contrary to state child care licensing requirements for the center.

A final constraint that may affect conducting collaborative research in the lab school is providing the time for faculty researchers and lab school teachers to hold meetings to brainstorm research ideas, plan studies or methods, or to reflect on the results of the project and how they can be applied. Faculty researchers, while busy, tend to have more flexible schedules than lab school teachers, who are responsible for the daily instruction and care of a group of children in the classroom. Lab school teachers must have support from program administration to schedule appropriate time to allow for meetings and discussions with faculty researchers. This is a key factor that enhances the research value of the lab school. If one mission of the lab school is to contribute significantly to research, program planning and budgeting must provide time for lab school staff to engage in research. Fortunately, the MCDLS teachers have daily preparation time as a part of their work day, which helps to facilitate time to meet with faculty to plan and conduct research. However, finding adequate time for meeting in collaboration teams may be challenging for some lab schools. Additionally, it may be difficult for lab school teachers to conduct some kinds of teacher-led research without release time from the classroom. At times it may be difficult for a teacher to engage in reflection or to conduct research when everyday classroom needs take precedence. For example, an incident occurred while a teacher and preschoolers were being video-recorded in the dramatic play area in the qualitative literacy study described above. Another child, not in the study, became ill and needed the classroom teacher's immediate attention. The video-recording had to stop, because the classroom teacher needed to meet the needs of the ill child. Understanding and flexibility are important in working with young children, by all members of a collaborative research team. In this situation the faculty researcher jumped in and helped by getting new clothes for the child while the teacher helped to change the child! While this constraint is not unique to collaborative research in lab schools, it is important for all members of the research team to understand that the health and well-being of the children are always the first priority.

The benefits of conducting collaborative lab school-based research are considerable. Faculty-led research can foster new insights, new information, and professional development opportunities for lab school teachers and university students. In the example provided involving the assessment of children's mathematical skills, laboratory school teachers were not involved in the leadership of the research project. However, the faculty researcher later returned and led professional development training with the lab school teachers that was focused on early childhood math. Consistent with an ADS approach, the faculty member's professional knowledge, lab-based research, and findings about early math learning and teaching were shared with the educators, thereby advancing their mathematics teaching practices with children.

A benefit of collaborative lab school research is the appeal research has for the professional teaching staff. The research focus of the lab school draws highly qualified teachers to the program and maintains the interest of the current teachers. For the classroom teachers, the possibility to participate in research engages them on a challenging intellectual level and nourishes their desire to learn and grow. As master teachers, they gain insights and perspectives through participation in research that advance their professional development in a deep and dynamic way. Participation in research contributes to the development of highly skilled professionals who set high standards for early childhood teaching. Knowledge is shared between teachers and faculty researchers, creating respectful collaborative professional exchanges and support. Just as expert faculty colleagues share their specialized knowledge with teachers, teachers share their theoretical and practical knowledge with the faculty. These kinds of interchanges can only facilitate best practices in an early childhood setting. The faculty who conduct research share their findings in scientific publications, and lab school teachers present their findings at local and national conferences and in practitioner-focused publications.

All research has both limitations and potential benefits within the particular context of each study. Lab schools provide opportunities to create an environment that is layered with teaching and learning opportunities. Children enrolled in a lab school benefit from the high quality program, the inquisitive enthusiasm of their teachers, and the rich learning experiences that are created and offered by the teachers. Teachers learn from and contribute to the learning and well-being of children, families, and co-workers. A unique learning opportunity in the lab school is presented by the teachers' participation in collaborative research with faculty. The impact of well-designed, collaborative, applied research in lab schools can be far reaching. The lab school program, the academic department, the community, and the early childhood field at large all benefit from good quality applied developmental research.

References

Abdal-Haqq, I. (1995). ERIC as a resource for the teacher researcher. ERIC Digest. Retrieved from http://www.ericdigests.org/1996-1/teacher.htm.

Bennett, L. M., Gadlin, H., & Levine-Finley, S. (2010). *Collaboration and team science: A field guide.* Washington, DC: National Institutes of Health.

Brauchla, M. (2013). Assessing feelings of hunger in preschool-aged children. Unpublished manuscript.

Britsch, S. (2015). Digital photography and science with ELs: Exploring science visually. 2015 Conference of Indiana Teachers of English to Speakers of Other Languages. Indianapolis, IN.

Brown, W. H., Googe, H. S., McIver, K. L., & Rathel, J. M. (2009). Effects of teacher-encouraged physical activity on preschool playgrounds. *Journal of Early Intervention, 31,* 126–145. doi: 10.1177/1053815109331858.

DeVellis, R. F. (2003). *Scale development: Theory and applications* (2nd ed.). Thousand Oaks, CA: Sage.

Gandini, L. (2008, October). Introduction to the fundamental values of the education of young children in Reggio Emilia. Retrieved from https://www.google.com/

webhp?sourceid=chrome-instant&ion=1&espv=2&ie=UTF-8#q=Introduction+to+ the+fundamental+values+of+te+education+of+young+childen+in+reggio+emilia.

Gold, Z. S., Elicker, J., Anderson, T., Choi, J. Y., & Brophy, S. P. (2015). Preschoolers' engineering play behaviors: Differences in gender and play context. *Children, Youth and Environments, 25*(3), 1–21. doi: 10.7721/chilyoutenvi.25.3.0001.

Han, A., & Hollich, G. (2013, April). Measuring children's eBook learning via iPad as compared to preferential looking. Poster presented at the Society for Research in Child Development, Seattle, WA.

Helm, J., & Katz, L. (2001). Young investigators: *The project approach in the early years.* New York: Teachers College Press.

Helmerhorst, K. O. W., Riksen-Walraven, J. M., Vermeer, H. J., Fukkink, R. G., & Tavecchio, L. W. C. (2014). Measuring the interactive skills of caregivers in child care centers: Development and validation of the Caregiver Interaction Profile Scales. *Early Education and Development, 25*, 770–790. doi: 10.1080/10409289.2014.840482.

Lerner, R. M., Wertlieb, D., & Jacobs, F. (2005). Historical and theoretical bases of Applied Developmental Science. In R. M. Lerner, F. Jacobs, & D. Wertlieb (Eds.), *Applied Developmental Science: An advanced textbook* (pp. 1–29). Thousand Oaks, CA: Sage.

McBride, B.A., Groves, M., Barbour, N., Horm, D., Stremmel, A., Lash, M., Bersani, C., Ratekin, C., Moran, J., Elicker, J., & Toussaint, S. (2012). Child Development Laboratory schools as generators of knowledge in early childhood education: New models and approaches. *Early Education and Development, 23*(2), 153–164. doi: 10.1090/10409289.2012.651068.

M-Chat. (2009, March 24). Retrieved from https://www.m-chat.org/mchat.php.

Mertens, D. M. (2010). *Research and evaluation in education and psychology: Integrating diversity with quantitative, qualitative, and mixed methods.* Thousand Oaks, CA: Sage.

Osborn, D.K. (1991). *Early childhood education in historical perspective* (3rd ed.). Athens, GA: Education Associates.

Purpura, D.J., & Napoli, A. R. (2015). Early numeracy and literacy: Untangling the relation between specific components. *Mathematical Thinking and Learning, 17*, 197–218.

Richardson, S. E., & Bofferding, L. (2015). Through their eyes: Early childhood teachers as learners and teachers of mathematics. In T. G. Bartell, K. N. Bieda, R. T. Putnam, K. Bradfield, & H. Dominguez (Eds.), *Proceedings of the 37th Annual Meeting of the North American Chapter of the International Group for the Psychology of Mathematics Education* (pp. 804–811). East Lansing, MI: Michigan State University.

Scales, B., Perry, J., & Tracy, R. (2012). Creating a classroom of inquiry at the University of California at Berkeley: The Harold E. Jones Child Study Center. *Early Education and Development, 23*, 165–180. doi: 10.1080/10409289.2012.651198.

The Center for Child and Family Studies (2015). Recent and ongoing research at CCFS. Retrieved from http://ccfs.ucdavis.edu/current_research.html.

Wilcox-Herzog, F., & McLaren, M. (2012). Lessons learned: Building a better laboratory school. *NALS Journal, 4*(3), 1–8. Retrieved from http://digitalcommons.ric.edu/nals/vol4/iss1/3.

5

BUILDING AND SUSTAINING COMMUNITY-BASED PARTNERSHIPS

Andrew J. Stremmel, Jennifer Kampmann, and Jill Thorngren

Unlike preschool programs and child care centers, university child development laboratory schools are unique and often refined and purified learning environments designed to be places for research, professional preparation, and service in their community contexts. As such, they are distinctively positioned to address the divide between research, policy, and early childhood practice (Elicker & Barbour, 2012). University laboratory schools exist primarily to serve as models for the application of child developmental theories, psychological principles, and educational practice. At best, they facilitate and support students' integration of theory and research and the demonstration, testing, and evaluation of new ideas and learned concepts.

Consistent with an applied developmental science (ADS) approach (Lerner, Jacobs, & Wertlieb, 2005; McBride et al., 2012), we believe that the lab school experience should extend beyond the university lab school building and into the community, and from the community into the lab school. Accordingly, the lab school becomes an educating community for both children and adults, and a workshop for applied developmental science wherein early childhood education students can better prepare for careers working with diverse children and families and engage in relevant research opportunities. Moreover, sustained professional development for those already teaching can be provided based on the best science regarding what and how to teach young children (see Barnett, 2003).

Although there has been an increase in a commitment to developing university–community partnerships, university lab schools and community-based programs still tend to view themselves as dissimilar worlds, one the "ivory tower" of theory and research and the other the "real world" of education and practice (Bullough, 2005; Stremmel, Hill, & Fu, 2003). In this chapter we address the question:

How can lab schools work together with community-based programs to address and study real-world problems of education and practice? We begin with the supposition that university lab schools are indeed viable venues for developing knowledge that can be applied to problems in the real world (Frank, 1962; Lerner, Jacobs, & Wertlieb, 2005). In particular, we discuss how the Fishback Center for Early Childhood Education at South Dakota State University (SDSU) has made efforts to create partnerships with community schools and agencies to better enable the Brookings, SD community to provide high quality care and education to its children, while supporting research that can illuminate both educational practice and an understanding of children's development in various contexts. We share some of the difficulties and challenges we faced in creating and sustaining university laboratory school-community partnerships, along with the opportunities such partnerships afford.

Historical Context of the Fishback Center for Early Childhood Education

The child development laboratory school has a rich history with a beginning that dates back 88 years to 1928, when Helen Young, a faculty member in the Department of Home Economics, established a play group for child development majors to observe and interact with young children. In 1929, the play group became an established preschool. From its inception, the lab school has existed to: 1) prepare early childhood education and human development majors to work effectively with young children and their families; and 2) provide a quality educational environment for children within a laboratory setting. Though it was an expectation that students learn with and from children in the lab school, it was much later that the lab school would become a place for conducting research and reflective inquiry.

Today, the Fishback Center is philosophically grounded in a Reggio-inspired, inquiry-based approach, which is consistent with and supported by an applied developmental science (ADS) approach to our research mission. Our vision is to create and nurture a learning community in which students and faculty see themselves as teacher–researchers, change agents, activists, and reflective thinkers, who study teaching practices and the experiences of children in systematic ways in order to solve daily classroom problems and improve educational processes within the classroom. In essence we believe that the lab school should be a place where theories and ideas are demonstrated and researched, and where new knowledge about children and practice are generated. Both a Reggio-inspired, inquiry approach and the ADS approach focus on the importance of rigorous and reflective inquiry, and the idea that theory, research, and practice are complementary and reciprocal. We believe that teachers must constantly examine and reflect on their understandings, possessing an attitude of research or inquiry, a disposition of curiosity, and the desire to know or understand. The effective teacher must search for sense and meaning in children's activity. In this instance, theory and practice are placed in a relationship of reciprocity, not in the traditional relationship of practice as consequent to theory.

Forming Partnerships

While the Fishback Center provides an excellent setting for education and clinical placement in the laboratory preschool and kindergarten classrooms, we increasingly seek to provide our prospective teachers with authentic field-based experiences outside of the center, in order to learn and critically examine as much as they can about teaching and learning. Since 2012, the Early Childhood Education faculty has been intentional about working to form new partnerships with three community agencies, in particular: the Brookings School District, Boys and Girls Club, and United Living Community (which fosters intergenerational relationships between elders and young children in a co-located intergenerational environment). Expanding our lab school to other community settings through creating collaborative partnerships is in full alignment with our university and college strategic plans and helps to meet the increasing need for adequate placements for university students majoring in Early Childhood Education and other human service disciplines. In line with accreditation standards and promising practices, early childhood education majors are required to complete three professional semesters that incorporate clinical experiences. Moving beyond the traditional one semester of student teaching, teacher candidates are now also required to engage in a full-year residency experience that allows for extended, focused field experiences in the final year of teacher preparation. Moreover, feedback from our students during senior exit interviews as well as from employers in the community has suggested that students need experiences in more diverse settings to gain the knowledge, skills, and dispositions necessary for them to better connect course content to "real-world" experiences. Creating extended laboratory experiences within the Brookings community allows us to provide our students with not only the required hours of clinical experience, but also the opportunity to experience diversified placements. Finally, placement of students in these extended laboratory settings enables us to contribute to the professional knowledge base by expanding the scope and depth of research and scholarly activity.

As we will discuss shortly, we have experienced various levels of success in working with community agencies. We have had some devastating setbacks as well as some promising collaborations. Consequently, we will discuss some of the lessons learned in our efforts to build collaborative partnerships with these programs. All three partnerships are in different stages of formation, and there is much work to be done.

Three Cases

1. The United Living Community Child Development Center: An Unsuccessful Venture

In 2012, with the support of a major community donor, SDSU was offered an opportunity to explore the possibility of creating a satellite lab school in the Child Development Center (CDC) at the United Living Community (ULC). The CDC offers child care for infants through preschool age children and is co-located at the ULC. Originally a center for independent and assisted living and a provider of respite care for seniors, the ULC added an intergenerational approach to elder care in 2001, posing a unique opportunity for regular supervised contact between children in the CDC and elders in the residential community. The ULC Child Development Center also holds the distinction of being the first intergenerational child development center to be certified by the National Association for the Education of Young Children (NAEYC) in 2005. However, this certification has since lapsed and one of the shared goals of our proposed university partnership was to help the CDC to again achieve NAEYC accreditation and become one of the few high quality, accredited educational programs in the state. To regain accreditation, additional staffing was necessary and our proposal was created to enable us to manage the operation of the center and hire the staff needed to bring the center up to the NAEYC accreditation level once again.

Our proposed collaboration also had the common goal to strengthen and further develop a rich intergenerational relationship with the elders at the ULC, while enabling our students to gain experiences and understanding related to intergenerational exchanges and programming. Faculty and students would also benefit from increased opportunities to further their research on infants due to a lack of infant classrooms in our current lab school program. Furthermore, faculty with expertise in child and adult development across two departments in our college (i.e. Teaching, Learning and Leadership, and Counseling and Human Development) would have the unique opportunity of conducting research related to intergenerational relationships and human development.

The potential for creating authentic partnerships can only be realized when partners come together to talk about the possibilities and challenges and address the hard questions. It was essential, therefore, that all stakeholders understand the needs of each partner and to try to find ways to collaboratively meet those needs. In the case of this partnership, we began with developing a formal letter of intent summarizing the process and principal terms of the proposed partnership in connection with the organization, operation, evaluation, and funding of the CDC, with ownership of the building remaining with United Living Community, management of the facility by South Dakota State University, and funding provided by the donor (a prominent local business). Next, a vision paper was prepared by university faculty, including the Dean of Education and Human Sciences (third author), detailing a rationale for creating this partnership and benefits to the center, the community, the donor, and university, along with staffing plans, enrollment goals, a proposed budget, and other relevant topics to ensure that the plan was viable and in the best interests of the children and elders on the ULC campus. It was absolutely critical that the mission of providing intergenerational activities would not be lost, but strengthened. The vision paper was submitted to the donor's foundation board for review and approval, followed by the same review and approval of the ULC Board of Directors. Additionally, university administration prepared a paper specifically detailing the academic benefits to students and faculty to obtain their support.

Although university administration originally had supported the proposal to move management of the CDC at the United Living Center to the university and become an extended laboratory campus housed in the College of Education and Human Sciences, it was not approved by our Board of Regents. A number of reasons were cited for this denial. First and foremost was the mission of our land-grant institution. While service and outreach are an integral part of what we do, managing a business, even a not-for-profit, is not a key component of our mission. Engaging in a management contract of this nature was viewed as stepping outside the scope of our services. There were also numerous personnel issues. Employees of the CDC would either be state employees, which triggered numerous approvals for additional staff lines accompanied by a significant increase in costs, or the CDC employees were classified as non-state employees thus creating different standards of treatment. Neither option was deemed acceptable.

Initially we were discouraged because we believed that the proposed partnership was innovative and much good faith effort by university administration, ECE faculty, and board of regent staff was invested in exploring the possibility of developing this satellite school partnership. But, ultimately the decision was made to forego incorporating the CDC into our program. We then stepped back and worked with the donor and the CDC to develop an alternative plan whereby a private child care provider firm took over management of the CDC. This allowed SDSU to remain involved in providing professional development opportunities for staff and the newly managed center was still a viable option for placement of our ECE students.

This was an interesting process as one of our newly hired instructors had recently left the private firm that was ultimately retained. He was able to step in and work with the donor to help negotiate appropriate terms and to advocate for our faculty being involved in ongoing professional development and supervision of students who will be placed at the site. Currently, students have been placed in the center to have more experiences with infants and toddlers, and many of the principles of the Reggio approach (e.g. documentation of children's experiences) have been demonstrated and supported, providing opportunities to synthesize theory and research and apply educational principles and developmental concepts espoused in the Fishback Center.

Our unsuccessful attempt gave us time to reflect on some important lessons learned. We learned a lot about financial models and how they differ between public universities and private businesses. Even with generous private support, universities must consider issues around the expansion of FTE, healthcare benefits (which differ drastically between public/private sectors), liability risk management, and employment classification. While the CDC was provided with a generous subsidy by a philanthropic donor and was never intended to be for-profit, running a business still conflicted with the primary missions of teaching, research, and service associated with our land-grant university.

We also realized that the question of how best to develop shared understandings related to philosophy, curriculum, and teacher preparation required ongoing dialogue and opportunities for professional development. The CDC teachers did not all share the same pedagogical skills, developmental understandings, and dispositions of university faculty; and faculty had to be open to learning from, and adopting the understandings of, CDC staff. We knew that questions had to be addressed such as, "How will current practices with which university faculty may not agree be discussed?" "When will time and space be made available to create common program goals, shared definitions, and consistent expectations so that, for example, teachers can help students make connections between what they are learning in university coursework and observing and doing in the CDC classrooms?" "How will research be conducted and what internal review process be put in place?" "What resources, support, and skill development will be required so that quality research can be conducted?" These are only some of the questions that we faced as we continue to move forward with other collaborations. They are important, as they have been helpful in guiding our present work.

2. The Brookings School District, Dakota Prairie Elementary School: A Hopeful Endeavor

Phil Jackson (1990) has suggested that laboratories, by definition, are unique settings in several ways. As stated earlier they are rarified environments, unlike schools, and students especially view them as idealistic and inconsistent with the real world of teaching. After all, schools to a much greater extent must deal with standards of learning, accountability assessments, and maintaining control, things which require the teacher's primary attention; and typically school classrooms have only one teacher for as many as 25 or more children.

Since 2004, the Brookings School District has partnered with SDSU to offer a kindergarten classroom in the Fishback Center. In 2013, the school district's decision to plan for the development of a new K-3 elementary school afforded another opportunity to collaborate and begin a dialogue with school partners about how the new school might become an extended laboratory site for our early childhood education students. The hope was to adopt a shared philosophy, one consistent with the Fishback Center's Reggio-inspired, inquiry-based approach, and to enable early childhood teacher candidates to co-teach with mentor teachers and better integrate theory and practice through research to help foster student learning and achievement. Learning from previous mistakes, the first and third authors met with school administration, including the superintendent, elementary principals, and curriculum director, to discuss how we could work together to create a mutually beneficial relationship and meet the needs of all learners (children, students, teachers, and parents).

Initial discussion included incorporating observation rooms and rooms designed for adult learning as well as children's learning. To further explore this idea of an extended lab school, faculty and administrators from the school district and university traveled to St Louis to visit a program that had been successful in developing a university-school partnership using a similar philosophy. One outcome was the formation of a steering committee of community members and school and university teachers and faculty to discuss shared purposes, common definitions, and consistent expectations for teaching and teacher preparation. A second outcome was the formation of a small committee (of which the first author was a member) to discuss creating an outdoor learning environment that would allow teachers to extend the curriculum outdoors and bring the outdoor curriculum indoors. In addition to typical outdoor activities and equipment, consideration was given to outdoor spaces that foster small group exploration, experimentation, and engagement in meaningful learning.

The school opened its doors in fall 2015 with many of the recommendations from our meetings coming to fruition. These include technology to facilitate both on- and off-site observations, space for small group work outside the classroom, opportunities for inquiry learning both indoors and outdoors, and rooms designed for adult learning and professional development as well as children's learning. Because of the successful design of this school, the third author of this chapter, who is the college dean, was asked to sit on a community-wide planning task force to help determine the scope and type of space needed across the entire school district in the next ten years. Monthly meetings now occur between the dean of our college and the newly hired superintendent of the school district. Collaborations continue to be fostered between the college and district as opportunities for ongoing professional development between faculty and teachers are implemented and feedback from the district is utilized in our ongoing cycle of continuous improvement. These opportunities include regular Friday afternoon gatherings of university and school faculty (led by the first author) to discuss mentoring and other aspects of teacher education; the development of a graduate (master's cohort) to develop teacher–leaders who will also serve as clinical educators; and regular discussions of our philosophy and joint vision for the kindergarten program and the ongoing development of teachers across their professional lives.

Schools that have done the best job of narrowing the achievement gap and delivering the best instruction have provided opportunities for sustained professional learning and development involving school teachers, university educators, and community citizens, as well as ongoing dialogue among university and school faculty (Feiman-Nemser, 2012). Especially when thinking about how to foster an innovative problem-based or community-based program, a primary aim should be to fashion the kind of school that best suits the entire community: teachers, parents, the physical setting, the citizens, and above all, the children.

3. The Boys and Girls Club: A Realized Collaboration

University faculty members also have been involved in the planning of an early childhood education expansion to the Boys and Girls Club (BGC) of Brookings since early 2013. Preschool expansion has been an important mission of the Club as very few full-day, center-based options for dual working families exist in the Brookings community. The expansion opened in early 2015, including the addition of four, full-day preschool classrooms and one junior kindergarten. In the spring of 2015, the BGC child development center was able to host two preschool student teachers from SDSU. In addition, one university faculty member (the second author) has been serving as a mentor for two of the centers' staff including doing observations and providing feedback for their professional development plans. The development of a new child development center at the Brookings Boys and Girls Club has afforded opportunities for new placements for our students and the fostering of professional development links between our lab school staff and Club staff. In particular, there is an opportunity to develop a common program philosophy and curriculum, while helping students to see different ways of implementing ideas and concepts that are often thought of as being unrealistic and non-transferable to other settings.

Collaborative planning between university faculty and Club staff was crucial to creating an extended laboratory setting for young children and adults, an educational environment that encouraged inquiry-based learning and a place to carry out research on learning and development, and a demonstration site for the application of developmental principles and methods of educational practice. To date, the sharing in teacher preparation opportunities has benefited the organization and university. Because the Boys and Girls Club serves children from preschool-age through eighteen, there are many new opportunities for teacher education candidates to gain practical experience and apply understanding of child and adolescent development, guidance, curriculum planning and assessment, administration, and program development. Observations, active learning, and co-teaching opportunities have been utilized through embedded, clinical experiences in teacher preparation courses.

Furthermore, the Boys and Girls Club of Brookings is the provider of summer enrichment programming for the Brookings, Volga, and Elkton School Districts. This programming provides educational enrichment for children in kindergarten through third grade who have been identified by their classroom teacher as being behind in reading and math. Many of these children are currently receiving special education services during the school year. In 2013, the second author was hired as a classroom teacher and program administrator to run the summer "PowerUp" program. This has provided her and other faculty with an opportunity to sharpen technical skills in practice, revisit and renew their own understandings of theory, and test and evaluate new ideas and concepts that will better enable them to work with teacher candidates. In 2015, an investment by the Sanford Education Consortium gave school counselors and counseling faculty an opportunity to participate in the summer program, further expanding services for children and clinical practice for faculty. Additionally, opportunities for early childhood education teacher candidates to co-teach alongside their professors in a clinical experience within a community setting has helped both see the value of extending professional learning beyond the traditional lab school building and into the community where teachers and students, adults and children have time within to reflect together, exchange ideas and perspectives, and evaluate learned concepts.

Challenges and Opportunities

Creating university–community partnerships is difficult because until the actual collaboration has begun, there is no way to predict what challenges may arise. This was certainly the case in our attempt to work with the ULC and manage their CDC program. Although we had placed students at the CDC to observe infants and toddlers on previous occasions, we really did not make efforts to work together in placing students at the site. In fact, neither the university nor our collaborating partners really knew that much about how to work together in developing common goals and shared understandings. What we have learned about the reality of university–community partnerships is that there are many layers of complexity to negotiate. Time, space, and commitment are necessary to dialogue about different perspectives and to develop mutual understandings and goals and consistent expectations. This means, among other things, that partners must make transparent their own values and assumptions, and be willing to confront their inadequacies and limitations. In making a commitment to form a partnership, both university and community-based partners are essentially agreeing to work together to learn from each other, to assume joint responsibility for preparing teachers and providing quality experiences for children.

Furthermore, we must continually ask, "Will our partners share the same commitment to research and discovery?" "If so, how do we work together to provide the conditions (e.g. skills, time, and resources) that will encourage a desire to develop and use inquiry to generate, apply, and disseminate knowledge gained from research?" Both partners have to give up some authority that comes from being positioned as experts (in the university "ivory tower" and in the "real world" of the community) and be willing to learn from one another what each has to offer. It means being willing to work toward the creation of a new participative community.

On the positive side, collaborative partnerships offer many opportunities. For one, they may be a great way to invigorate the lives of faculty, students, and community teachers and staff, and have access to one another's wisdom and expertise. Establishing community-based partnerships and collaborations may afford our students additional opportunities to synthesize theory and research and apply educational principles and developmental concepts espoused in the Fishback Center. These expanded laboratory settings enable students to observe children's development in a community setting as part of their course work; engage with faculty and teachers in systematic inquiry (teacher research) into problems of practice; and, they provide rich opportunities for collaborative research focused on issues and problems unique to a community setting and related to children's learning and development, teacher preparation, curriculum implementation, and classroom processes. Additionally, it may allow opportunities to involve both university and community faculty and staff in the collaborative planning of teacher education courses and curriculum, and the sharing of innovative teaching practices. University faculty and community-based teachers and staff may be better able to ensure that assignments connect; discuss assessments; observe each other's teaching; co-teach in both school and university classrooms; and develop professional learning communities (laboratory-embedded professional development) focused on the most pressing educational issues.

Final Thoughts

Strong communities are marked by a collective accountability for taking on the fundamental tasks of educating and caring for their children. Dynamic partnerships involving university lab schools and a variety of community partners may enable collaborative opportunities to identify real-world problems of practice and study them in a variety of contexts (Lerner, Jacobs, & Wertlieb, 2005). Extending the lab school into the community creates new settings for students and faculty to apply theories and principles of practice, ask questions based on observations of real-life problems, and conduct research and make recommendations that can influence the thinking and actions of community professionals. Accordingly the lab school in its broadest sense becomes a workshop for applied developmental science, where students learn through meaningful exploration and discovery and take part in both the generation and dissemination of new knowledge (McBride et al., 2012).

References

Barnett, W. S. (2003). Better teachers, better preschools: Student achievement linked to teacher qualifications. *Preschool Policy Matters, 2*. New Brunswick, NJ: NIEER.

Bullough, R. V. (2005). Being and becoming a mentor: School-based teacher educators and teacher educator identity. *Teaching and Teacher Education, 21*(2), 143–155.

Elicker, J., & Barbour, N. (2012). Introduction to the special issue: University laboratory schools in the 21st century. *Early Education and Development, 21*, 157–159. doi: 10.1080/10409289.2012.649665.

Feiman-Nemser, S. (2012). *Teachers as learners.* Cambridge, MA: Harvard Education Press.

Frank, L. K. (1962). The beginnings of child development and family life education in the 20th century. *Merrill-Palmer Research Quarterly of Applied Behavior and Development, 8*(4), 207–227.

Jackson, P. (1990). *Life in classrooms* (Rev. ed.). New York: Teachers College Press.

Lerner, R. M., Wertlieb, D., & Jacobs, F. (2005). Historical and theoretical bases of Applied Developmental Science. In R. M. Lerner, F. Jacobs, & D. Wertlieb (Eds.), *Applied Developmental Science: An advanced textbook* (pp. 1–29). Thousand Oaks, CA: Sage.

McBride, B. A., Groves, M., Barbour, N., Horm, D., Stremmel, A., Lash, M., Bersani, C., Ratekin, C., Moran, J., Elicker, J., & Toussaint, S. (2012). Child Development Laboratory schools as generators of knowledge in early childhood education: New models and approaches. *Early Education and Development, 23*(2), 153–164.

Stremmel, A. J., Hill, L. T., & Fu, V. R. (2003). An inside perspective of paradigm shifts in child development laboratory programs: Bridging theory and professional preparation. In S. Reifel (Series Ed.), *Advances in Early Education and Day Care, 12.*

6

MAKING THE SHIFT FROM PRESCHOOL TO LABORATORY SCHOOL

A Case Example

Nancy E. Barbour, Reece Wilson, and Jennifer Ryan Newton

Change is both inevitable and hard. The story we will tell speaks to both. The task was to make the shift from a preschool program connected to a college of education to a potential inclusive early childhood education laboratory school ripe for Applied Developmental Science. As with any change, it is a work in progress. In order to provide the necessary context for this story, it is important to first explore the conceptual framework for such a shift. Understanding the history as prologue to the present provides a map for such a shift.

A Conceptual Framework

In the early part of the 20th century, efforts to understand the development of young children became a compelling endeavor across disciplines. Centers were established across the country, usually housed in universities, to engage in systematic research to build a knowledge base to improve and enhance the lives of children and families. What had been schools for the enrichment of young children became centers for studying and understanding child development and learning (NSSE Year Book, 1929). Early in the 1920s, economist Lawrence K. Frank was authorized to determine which university programs would receive Laura Spelman Rockefeller Memorial funding to engage in such child study. Frank's vision was that research should be done in interdisciplinary collaborations for the purpose of contributing to policies that improve lives (Lomax, 1977). The enactment of Frank's ideas resulted in "… a nationwide network of children's services, [that] created overnight a system of institutes of child welfare for the study of child development and promotion of parent education" (Senn, 1975, p. 12). The days of university laboratory settings for the study of child development were begun. Many of the preschool programs, often housed in Home Economics departments, were elevated to a place of scientific investigation.

Throughout the country, these newly focused child study settings were pro-liferating and engaging in research (NSSE Year Book, 1929). Over the course of almost 100 years, their purpose and practices have varied, but many of the insti-tutes established through Frank's work have endured. Three examples illustrate this point.

Gesell's early work at Yale University involved innovative techniques for pho-tographing and recording child development. The site has since evolved into the Yale Child Study Center, described as "a department at Yale University School of Medicine which brings together multiple disciplines to further the understand-ing of the problems of children and families" (http://childstudycenter.yale.edu/index.aspx).

The University of Minnesota began its operation under John Anderson, "founded in the belief that the scientific study of child development was essential to the promotion of child welfare" (http://www.cehd.umn.edu/icd/about/) and continues today with the same mission.

University of California, Berkeley's laboratory program began as the Institute of Child Welfare, under the leadership of Herbert Stolz and Harold Jones, as an inter-disciplinary setting to engage in the longitudinal study of infants and adolescents. Today, the University of California—Berkeley Institute for Human Development is an active site for the study of development across the lifespan.

Frank had an expectation of science that was disseminated and would lead to solutions for social problems, always with the expectation of rigorous investiga-tion (Frank, 1962). Many of these child study settings have changed over time to be places of research, professional preparation, and service in their community contexts. Change was inevitable and, at times, difficult, but these sites have con-tinued to be places of scientific inquiry.

Applied Developmental Science

Given the rich history of child development laboratory settings over the last cen-tury, we wondered whether these are still viable venues for developing knowl-edge that can be applied to solve real problems in the real world. As we wrestled with this question, we looked for a conceptual framework that would speak to these concerns. Applied Developmental Science is such a framework and provides fertile ground for considering both the essential elements of child development laboratory programs and the potential for research and practice to address current social issues.

Applied Developmental Science (ADS) is applied work, having direct impli-cations for children, families, policymakers, and practitioners. It is developmen-tal in that it is research done systematically and focused on people through the lifespan. It is science in that it requires rigorous research methods (Lerner, Jacobs, & Wertlieb, 2005). ADS has as its intended impact the improved life tra-jectories of the broad range of constituents served by this scholarship (Lerner,

Fischer, & Weinberg, 2000). Some of the features of ADS is **applied** in nature with direct implications for children, families, and policymakers. The **developmental** component addresses development across the lifespan and across contexts. The **science** component emphasizes intentional inquiry that leads to putting theory into practice (Lerner et al., 2000).

A Case in Point

Unlike some of the other child development laboratory programs that have been in operation over decades as sites for research, service, and professional preparation, the case in point is a traditional preschool program connected with a teacher preparation program. The journey that will be shared is used to illustrate the challenges and benefits of shifting practice in order to engage in ADS as a university laboratory setting. The potential was there to do applied work, having direct implications for children, families, policymakers, and practitioners.

The Beginning of the Shift

We, a faculty member and an administrator involved with the preschool program, saw an opportunity to maximize the potential of the Young Children's Program (YCP) as a model for practice and preparation when the director announced her retirement. Having discussed with the leadership team the need to increase the viability of the program, we began to conceptualize change. As we proposed the shift from preschool program to laboratory program, we paid attention to the qualities necessary to be a viable child development laboratory setting. The program would need a clearly defined mission and plan for addressing the mission. The mission, ideally, would need to be conceptualized as working toward the greater good of the community. There would need to be "hard," reliable funding we could count on for operation. We would need to have both opportunities and commitments for collaboration across the university resources. We would need strong leadership to guide the laboratory. We had to be mindful of the need to balance the three-part mission of research, service, and professional preparation. Finally, we had to be responsive to the community in which we resided, both university and local, in order to have faculty and administrative buy-in (Barbour, 2003).

The Young Children's Program has been in place at James Madison University for more than four decades as a half-day program for three and four year olds. It follows a curriculum that is described as developmentally appropriate and family-centered (http://www.jmu.edu/coe/ycp/index.shtml). It has great popularity among the community as it is focused on the child's developmental needs, includes pre-service teachers doing practicum experience, and has a low teacher–child ratio. The teachers have master's degrees, communicate regularly with families, and open their doors to visitation and observation. In short, it is a high quality setting, accredited by the National Association for the Education of Young Children (NAEYC). The teacher education programs in the College of Education include Early Childhood Education, Elementary Education, and Inclusive Early Childhood Education, all initial licensure programs that included practice with three and four year olds. Students from the Elementary Education program have been placed there regularly for field experience. The Inclusive Early Childhood Education teacher preparation program is the newest of the programs and we saw an opportunity to shift the Young Children's Program to become a model for Inclusive Early Childhood practices and a potential research site for faculty, so we approached the local school division to discuss a partnership. They were in need of spaces to provide services for three year olds who had been identified as having special needs. It was a natural step in the process of engaging in ADS—serving community needs and becoming a site for addressing and studying real, live research questions.

Year One

The first step was to develop this partnership with the local school division in order to offer slots for young children with special needs to attend our program. The city schools offer preschool services for four year olds who are at risk of delay or school failure through a state preschool initiative (Virginia Preschool Initiative). Consequently, four year olds who qualify for services under IDEA have services. However, three year olds who qualify are in need of placements. Lacking enough appropriate spaces for three year olds in the community, the division was interested in placing four children in the three-year-old morning classroom, making them 33 percent of the class population. The school division also assigned one of their Early Childhood Special Education teachers to the classroom to co-teach with our Early Childhood Education teacher. This was just the beginning of a domino effect, as we then needed to develop campus relationships with other programs that could provide the necessary support services (e.g. speech language therapy, occupational therapy). Of course, this entailed negotiations regarding the fee for services, supervision, and mutual benefits. This was a snag, as we thought there could be reciprocity for providing field sites for their students. In fact, we believed that the benefit that the Occupational Therapy students received by using the YCP as a practicum site would offset the service provided by them and their supervisor. However, this was not the commonly held view and they agreed to a limited offer of service, after which we shifted to services provided by the school division. Services from the Speech Language therapy center were a bit less complicated because one of the faculty in our college was certified to provide clinical supervision for the speech language students administering therapy in the YCP. Reciprocity across programs within the same university was not a reality.

Eventually that first year, under an interim faculty director, children arrived, services were delivered, and college students were participating. Had we achieved our goal of becoming a child development laboratory site in one-and-a-half semesters? We had relatively stable funding though not a clear vision of how we might increase or manage the funding for additional services or research. We were working on the collaborations across departments. We were responding to community needs. However, though we had a commitment to be an inclusive early childhood setting, we still needed a clearly known and understood mission and a fully funded tenure track position for a director as well as a clear research agenda. We had not found a balance for research, professional preparation, and service. Yet, we were well on our way to fulfilling these goals and the elements of ADS.

Year One: Lessons Learned

There were a number of lessons learned from the first year of this shift. As we considered what needed to be done to become a laboratory engaging in ADS, we became aware of some unanticipated tasks.

#1 Developing a Broad Base of Stakeholders

We needed to define our mission to a broader constituency of faculty, administrators, parents, and support service providers in order to develop buy-in from the school division, college, and university. As a result of a series of problem-solving situations, we learned that there was not a commonly understood philosophy of inclusive education. We saw a need to engage all stakeholders in dialogue about inclusion and what it meant for this preschool program. What was it that we wanted to model for our students?

#2 Developing Common Understandings Among Stakeholders

We learned that working across departments and disciplines requires deep, extensive conversations in order to develop consensus about practice. Each discipline brings different assumptions about how best to deliver service. Working in one setting with children requires mutual understanding about strategies, beliefs, and collaboration. In order to promote inclusive practices we had to be inclusive professionals. No one perspective served all of those involved in service delivery.

#3 Working Collaboratively Toward a Common Goal

We had to evaluate the curriculum and ensure all team members were knowledgeable about the theoretical foundations, curriculum content and model of instruction, instructional design features, assessment, and research base of the curricula used. We had to share resources that accurately expressed the professional philosophies of all involved and make sure to meet and discuss these ideas as a team.

#4 Encouraging Authentic Engagement of Faculty in the Laboratory Setting

Finally, we realized that we had not even come close to the goal of pulling faculty and students into the laboratory to do scientific investigation. We had to engage faculty and administration in discourse about their present and potential roles in the laboratory program. There was not a tradition of seeing the program as a resource for research and practice. This was essential for us if we were aiming toward a site for ADS.

As we looked at the structure of the program, noting the traditional half-day program operation, we wondered how responsive this was to the community. Likewise, this part-day operation had an impact on the funding. We struggled with the need to expand the operation to full-day services since this appeared to be a community need. The need to shift hours of operation and, subsequently, tuition proved to be a long and difficult process to accomplish. Consequently, the program remained as a half-day program for the next year of operation while we continued to establish our partnership with the local school division. A full-time, tenure track faculty member was hired to direct the YCP as 50 percent of his course load. He came with 20 years' experience as a university preschool director. Consequently, he was familiar with both the operation of a university-based preschool program and the necessary connections to the faculty and curriculum that maximize the potential as a laboratory setting.

Year Two: A New Director

As the newly hired director, his major focus for the first year was to begin guiding the program toward a laboratory school model, in both philosophy and practice. This meant moving from the traditional early childhood program to one that practiced the basic principles of a lab school program: providing high quality care and education for young children, preparing teachers and others (occupational therapists, speech language pathologists), generating research, and disseminating this research to families, communities, and others.

The director wondered how he could best achieve the necessary shift to make the program a laboratory site, incorporating these principles. He began by examining the school's mission statement. As Barbour (2003) states, "It is critical to have a clearly defined mission, a plan for addressing the mission, and a means for documenting accomplishments." (p. 28). How could a clearly defined mission statement best be crafted, and who should the stakeholders include, as we undertook this endeavor?

It was important to include teachers, families, and faculty in the process of developing a mission statement that reflected what we wanted our program to be. To this end, an open invitation was sent to every family in the program to be part of the parent advisory board. In addition, each teacher was encouraged to participate, as well as our department head and dean. It was explained to all that the work of this board for the year would be to develop both a mission statement and a values statement for the school. As we prepared to gather for the first meeting of the semester, the parent advisory board consisted of two fathers, every teacher, the department head, and the director. This was a core group that worked together for the remainder of the year.

As the work to develop a mission statement began, an expert in the process of developing both mission and values statements for programs was asked to act as a guide. After many meetings and other informal communications, a mission statement was crafted, as well as a values statement:

> **Mission Statement:** *The Young Children's Program provides a nurturing, diverse, and layered experience for children, families and JMU community by modeling and supporting the best practices to meet the unique needs of all learners.*

> **Values Statement:** *We collaborate with our community, leveraging support and access to quality resources, diverse skill sets, and a broadened knowledge base.*
>
> *We honor intentional experiences and interactions that provide a solid foundation for high quality early childhood education.*
>
> *We build positive, respectful, lasting relationships with our families, students and community partners.*
>
> *We believe that learning should be student-centered and built upon the needs and interests of all learners.*
>
> *We are an inclusive program where all students have the opportunity to be full and active participants.*

These statements regarding the mission and values as a school are a work in progress, and will be molded and changed as the program evolves. We feel there are some issues with vagueness in the mission statement and we wonder how widely known and understood the statement is. Particularly, we wonder if there is a clear meaning for the phrase "layered experience." Perhaps it is an attempt to convey the many and varied learning experiences that are part of the program. Revisiting these documents will be part of our future work as will our plans for addressing the mission and documenting our progress. We will also need to consider how this mission addresses the community outside of our university family.

In our efforts to move toward an ADS model, this will be an important part of our evolution.

Strong personnel and strong leadership are also essential for a viable laboratory school setting and a site capable of Applied Developmental Science. The new director was knowledgeable about the three-part mission of the lab school and especially about the need for professional development and accountability for the teachers. He offered them opportunities, both in-house and external to the university, for professional development experiences. In this way, the teachers began to see the critical nature of their roles in professional preparation and the need for them to share their knowledge of curriculum development and planning with the teacher education students by sharing their planning process and their knowledge of families and children. This also added to their sense of ownership of the laboratory setting.

Another piece of our future and current work that relates to the mission involves building upon the partnership with the various stakeholders/service providers. Central to this work is building relationships and collaborating across disciplines. One of our most successful collaborative endeavors has been with the faculty and students in the communication disorders department. Specifically, students studying speech language pathology (SLP) participate in the YCP program. The students in this program are gaining valuable knowledge as they work with our teachers, children, and families. Many of these students have never been in an early childhood setting. Thus, important ideas such as being at the children's level for effective communication, or using person-first language are new concepts. These students are able to practice skills, theory, and concepts taught in class, while at the same time helping all children increase their language skills.

The students in the SLP program work in the school two mornings each week. They deliver services with the guidance of their faculty supervisors. One supervisor is from the communications disorders department, and the other supervisor is a faculty member in the educational foundations and exceptional education department (EFEX). Supervisors, teachers, and SLP clinicians work closely both in and out of the classroom. Regular meetings are held with those people delivering service on Fridays. Concerns are shared and discussed, and positive outcomes are celebrated. This routine has solved some of the issues experienced in the first year where stakeholders from different disciplines found themselves speaking "different" languages and at cross purposes.

Other collaborations that we are undertaking and growing include working with occupational therapy students who are observing and interacting with all children. Though in the past these students did provide services under the guidance of a faculty member in the Occupational Therapy department, they are not delivering services at the current time as there are no children with Individual Educational Plans who require occupational therapy.

We also have students from the music program. The school director and a member of the EFEX department recruit these students in their university course. The program philosophy is explained, as well as topics such as developmentally appropriate practice and strategies for working with young children. These students, under the guidance of their university instructor, then plan and provide learning experiences for the children. Also out of the music department, there is a faculty in residence who provides professional development for teachers and students. This faculty member also interacts with children and families by engaging in learning experiences with children and by being a guest speaker at parent night meetings. These collaborations with students and faculty seem to be positive steps in involving many entities in meaningful, community experiences.

A central focus of the director's work during the past year has been to generate more faculty interest and involvement in research at the YCP. This piece has been limited, but bridges are being built to increase involvement in this area. Developing a collegial, friendly rapport with all members of our department is central to this work. Through email and face-to-face conversations, faculty have been encouraged to actively participate in the life of the school. These personal connections are beginning to show promise. This is the first step to the kind of intellectual exchange regarding professional preparation, research, and service to the community that is the lifeblood of a laboratory school. For instance, there are several faculty members teaching early childhood courses that bring their classes to the YCP for the purpose of examining and discussing the physical environment and its effect on learning. Several other faculty have created assignments for their courses in which students schedule observation times in order to observe children and teachers, and relate observations to course material. These are small steps that get closer to the strong connection needed among personnel, professional preparation, and the laboratory program.

One aspect that is particularly exciting is the beginning of research being conducted at the school by faculty members. Several members of the reading program, along with the director, are beginning a research project involving digital literacy in the preschool classroom. Likewise, the YCP teachers are also involved in research at their school. Faculty are working on a study of STEM education in the early childhood classroom, and what that looks like in their classrooms. The research has also reached the point of dissemination at local conferences. These changes are small, indeed, but are evidence of shifts in the culture in that: 1) the site is viewed as a viable research site; and 2) that faculty and YCP teachers are beginning to see the potential for the site to be a place of scientific inquiry.

Year Two: Lessons Learned

Perhaps the most important lesson learned is that we were indeed in need of a full-time faculty director. This means that there is a tenure level faculty member whose role is 50 percent teaching/scholarship/service and 50 percent director; someone with the potential for job security and an obligation to engage in scholarship. The dedicated time and effort proved quite productive in creating some of the basic structures like a mission statement, an active advisory committee, and faculty buy-in. The sustained work with the teachers, families, and faculty has started a small groundswell of connection between the YCP and the university community. There is still much to be done for the YCP to realize the potential as a laboratory school and site for ADS. In particular, the potential for ADS that explores the challenges and innovations in the field of Inclusive Early Childhood Education has not been tapped at all. There are many research questions looming about the phenomenon and the YCP has the practice occurring right now. In fact, the future holds great promise. The partner school division has agreed to establish an additional preschool classroom for young children from economically disadvantaged homes in the YCP space, adding another layer of inclusion. It will be a full-day program and will be done collaboratively with the College of Education.

Ideas to Ponder

The story of this shift in practice leaves us with a number of important ideas to ponder and consider as we think about the process of becoming a laboratory school that embodies the necessary characteristics to engage in Applied Developmental Science, perhaps even as part of a larger consortium of laboratory schools.

- Change is hard; change is slow; change takes more than wishing it so.
- Collaboration across disciplines means you must be able to see and value others' points of view.
- You need to be an active, engaged listener.
- Collaboration across disciplines means you need to be knowledgeable about the professional standards of those disciplines.
- Relationships are everything; build them, foster them, and nurture them.
- Stakeholders must be able to model, facilitate, and advance the learning of pre-service teachers.
- It is necessary to develop an administrative structure that is clear and accessible to all stakeholders.
- Have a plan for addressing conflict.
- Share the mission and values of the program widely.
- Don't assume anything; make the roles and responsibilities of all members clear.
- Be clear from the beginning about goals and accountability.

- Keep communication open and often.
- Nurture the process of inquiry and reflection; pose tough research questions.

This case in point, in some ways, lays bare the bones of what it means to be a high quality child development laboratory setting. We began from the basics. Still to be assessed is how we create an environment that invites and supports collaborative research that focuses on contextual, cultural, embedded lifespan issues. And we have yet to consider the many benefits to be had from being part of a larger consortium.

Conclusion

Change is not only inevitable and hard, but it is also very slow. The journey toward becoming a lab school is still in progress. Will the YCP become a larger, full day inclusive program with more classrooms and teachers? Will the partner school division become a stronger and more active stakeholder? Is there will in the college and the university to become a model, inclusive early childhood program, engaged in Applied Developmental Science? These questions are the path to the rest of the story.

References

Barbour, N. E. (2003). The early history of child development laboratory programs. In B. A. McBride & N. E. Barbour (Eds.), *Advances in Early ducation and Day Care, Vol. 12. Bridging the gap between theory, research, and practice: The role of child development laboratory programs in early childhood education* (pp. 9–29). Oxford, UK: Elsevier.

Frank, L. K. (1962). The beginnings of child development and family life education in the twentieth century. *Merrill-Palmer Research Quarterly of Applied Behavior and Development, 8*(4), 207–227.

James Madison University. (2015). Young children's program. Retrieved December 17, 2015, from http://www.jmu.edu/coe/ycp/index.shtml

Lerner, R. M., Fisher, C. B., & Weinberg, R. A. (2000). Toward a science for and of the people: Promoting civil society through the application of developmental science. *Child Development, 71*, 11–20.

Lerner, R. M., Wertlieb, D., & Jacobs, F. (2005). Historical and theoretical bases of Applied Developmental Science. In R. M. Lerner, F. Jacobs, & D. Wertlieb (Eds.), *Applied Developmental Science: An advanced textbook* (pp. 1–29). Thousand Oaks, CA: Sage.

Lomax, E. (1977). The Laura Spelman Rockefeller Memorial: Some of its contributions to early research in child development. *Journal of the History of the Behavioral Sciences, 13*, 283–293.

NSSE (National Society for the Study of Education) (1929). *The National Society for the Study of Education twenty-eighth yearbook: Preschool and parent education.* Bloomington, IN: Public School Publishing Company.

Senn, M. J. E. (1975). Insights on the child development movement in the United States. *Monographs of the Society for Research in Child Development, 40*(3–4 Serial No. 161), 1–107.

University of Minnesota. (2014). University of Minnesota Institute of Child Development: About the institute. Retrieved March 11, 2014, from http://www.cehd.umn.edu/icd/about

Yale University. (2014). Yale University School of Medicine Child Study Center: Our history. Retrieved March 11, 2014, from http://childstudycenter.yale.edu/index.aspx

7

EDUCARE AS A MODEL OF MULTI-SITE, COLLABORATIVE, POLICY-RELEVANT RESEARCH

Diane M. Horm

The purpose of this chapter is to describe two key processes embraced by Educare, an enhanced Head Start/Early Head Start program, with the goal of informing cross-site, collaborative, applied research. The two processes are: (1) common data collection across multiple sites, and (2) use of data to impact program and policy at multiple levels. Educare's "lessons learned" through implementing these two processes will be shared to inform the formation and implementation of a research consortium of lab schools. Although Educare is not a university-based laboratory school, its focus on combining robust, embedded research with the delivery of a high-quality comprehensive child and family development program designed for children and families living in poverty is an example of Applied Developmental Science (ADS) (Lerner, Jacobs, & Wertlieb, 2003, 2005) in action that has important implications for building and analyzing databases to answer the most relevant contemporary program- and policy-oriented questions related to early care and education.

Research in Lab Schools: One Example

As highlighted in this book and other sources (e.g. see McBride & Barbour, 2003), university lab schools have generated, applied, and disseminated knowledge to inform practice in early childhood education since their inception in the early 20th century. As a former lab school director, along with the staff at the University of Rhode Island (URI) Child Development Centers, we embraced the three-fold mission of teaching, research, and service common across contemporary university-based lab schools. Working together as a staff we excelled in teaching by providing high-quality pre-service professional preparation to our college students and extensive service/outreach by engaging in productive professional development collaborations with a range of partners including the state department of education, state early childhood professional associations, public schools, and other community-based groups and agencies (see Horm & Warford, 2003). While we were strong in teaching and service/outreach, our research activities were not as robust or comprehensive. Although we did engage in research, the scope was generally limited to URI faculty and graduate students who implemented their independently designed studies in our two locations and shared their findings through conference presentations and publications in professional journals. While this research activity and the resulting new knowledge often informed our practice, it generally did not have a direct impact on children and families outside our two sites of the URI Child Development Centers. Based on experience and conversations with other lab school staff, this scenario is not unique. Research implemented in university-based lab schools is typically designed and conducted by individual researchers, or small research teams, who rightfully take advantage of the university-affiliated lab school to host their work. While this is aligned with the research mission of lab schools, the researchers often work in relative isolation and may or may not address research questions that have direct relevance for practice or policy. Additionally, due to the study being conducted in only one university-affiliated lab school, the researchers must typically acknowledge limitations in their sample sizes and sample demographic characteristics that limit the generalizability of findings and associated impacts in the practice and policy arenas.

Educare as an Alternative Model

The growing network of Educare Schools can serve as a model of how multiple program sites and their affiliated researchers can collaborate to build a common research agenda and by working together can overcome the problems noted above to have a significant impact on both program and policy decisions, without giving up the local use of data. After a brief description of the history, growth, and features of the Educare program model, focused attention will be placed on the roles of applied research and data use in this model.

Educare

Educare is a comprehensive early childhood education program model designed to serve young children, birth to age five, and their families who live in poverty (Educare Learning Network [ELN], 2015). The model was developed by the Ounce of Prevention Fund who, in collaboration with Chicago Public Schools and the Irving Harris Foundation, opened the first Educare in Chicago in 2000. In 2016, a total of 21 Educare Schools are in operation across the United States in communities as diverse as Tulsa, Seattle, Miami-Dade, Washington DC, and Central Maine. For a listing of all Educare sites and more information about Educare, see www.educareschools.org.

Educare describes itself as a program, place, partnership, and platform for change. Specifically, "local public-private *partnerships* create and support an Educare school—the *place*—following the Educare model—the *program*—which serves as a *platform* for broader policy and systems change" (Yazejian, Bryant, & Kennel, 2013, p. 209). Relative to the program, Educare meets the Head Start and Early Head Start performance standards and goes beyond them (Yazejian et al., 2013) by implementing a variety of enhancements including: year-round, full-day services; lead teachers with bachelor's degrees; intensive, ongoing embedded professional development; family support staff with limited caseloads and bachelor's-level training; a Research Program Partnership with local researchers joining with each site's Educare program staff to tailor continuous improvement planning and data use; and contribution of local data to a cross-site Educare Implementation Study.

In each Educare location, public–private partnerships develop to fund and implement the program. Federal guidance and funds from Early Head Start and Head Start form the base for programming and funding, with local, state, and philanthropic sources augmenting both programming and funding (ELN, 2015) to support enhancements such as the full-day, year-round schedule and highly qualified, degreed staff. In addition to serving as a model of how early childhood programs can be created and sustained in communities, Educare schools serve as "showrooms" demonstrating the delivery of high-quality early childhood services (ELN, 2015). Relative to classroom quality, Educare classrooms demonstrate significantly higher overall quality as measured by the Infant/Toddler Environment Rating Scale (ITERS-R) (Harms, Cryer, & Clifford, 2006) and the Early Childhood Environment Rating Scale (ECERS-R) (Harms, Clifford, & Cryer, 2005) than results reported for other infant/toddler and preschool classrooms in published large-scale studies (Yazejian & Bryant, 2012). For example, in 2012 the average cross-site ITERS-R and ECERS-R scores were 5.8, falling in the range defined as high quality (Yazejian, Bryant, Freel, Burchinal, & ELN Investigative Team, 2015). Similarly, results on the Classroom Assessment Scoring System (CLASS) PreK (Pianta, LaParo, & Hamre, 2008) fell in the high to moderately high range with an average cross-site score of 6.4 for emotional support, 5.7 for classroom organization, and 3.5 for instructional support (Yazejian et al., 2015). As noted by Yazejian and Bryant (2012), Educare's average instructional support scores are above the threshold required for children's acquisition of academic skills and higher than averages reported in other studies of early childhood programs. Individual Educare sites review their ITERS, ECERS, and CLASS results as one source of information to inform their professional development planning and efforts at continuous program improvement.

As noted above, the Educare model embraces the collection and use of data and the partnership with local researchers as key features. The goal is for the local researcher to be "embedded" as part of the program (Yazejian et al., 2013). In fact, the Educare logic model identifies four core program features with data utilization listed first and recognized as driving and informing the other three—embedded professional development, high-quality teaching practices, and intensive family engagement. The implementation of these core features, with the emphasis on the primacy of data and its use, is predicted to prepare young children, birth to five years, growing up in poverty, for kindergarten as well as longer-term academic and life success (ELN, 2015). More details on the Educare model and its implementation can be found in published reports (e.g. Guss, Norris, Horm, Monroe, & Wolfe, 2013; Stein, Freel, Hanson, Pacchiano, & Eiland-Williford, 2013; Yazejian et al., 2013; Yazejian et al., 2015).

The emphasis on data and its use distinguishes Educare from other early education programs. Each Educare site forms a partnership with a researcher, typically from a local university, to conduct the required Educare Implementation Study. This partnership is called the Research Program Partnership (RPP) and is charged to implement a reciprocal data feedback and utilization cycle (Stein et al., 2013) to inform local program improvement. Thus, like quality lab schools, the voices of practitioners and researchers are evident; and similar to the tenets of Applied Developmental Science the problems of practice inform the research questions that are posed as well as the data collection methods and strategies.

Since 2005, the local researchers affiliated with each Educare site, called Local Evaluation Partners or LEPs, have been coordinated by a team from the FPG Child Development Institute at the University of North Carolina at Chapel Hill, led by Noreen Yazejian and Donna Bryant, who are referred to as the National Evaluation Partner (NEP). Together the NEPs and LEPs have designed a common set of measures, in collaboration with Educare program partners, that are administered on a common schedule with the NEP ensuring quality control through common training as well as regular reliability and accuracy monitoring. The Educare Implementation Study includes direct child assessments, staff surveys, parent interviews, and classroom observations. This coordination allows data to be aggregated across sites, resulting in large databases. To date, analyses have demonstrated the high quality of the programs (briefly summarized above) and shows that children who are enrolled earlier, and for longer periods of time, demonstrate better outcomes (Yazejian et al., 2015). This large-sample, "practical" research has caught the attention of other researchers as well as policymakers and funders.

What Lessons can Educare Offer to University-based Lab School Research Consortia?

The above description of Educare shows it shares some common features with university-based lab schools. These include:

- Emphasis on the delivery of high-quality, research-informed services to young children and their families;
- Use as a "showroom" or observations site where others can see high-quality services in action on a daily basis;

- Emphasis on ongoing professional development;
- Affiliation and partnership with local university-based researchers.

A major difference is the intentional design and implementation of a network to facilitate cross-site data collection and use. The Educare network has negotiated a common set of child, family, staff, and classroom measures; common protocols for training and assessment administration; common timelines for data collection; and common approaches to data management and analysis. This collaboration has resulted in a large and diverse database that enables the framing of research questions to address numerous policy-relevant questions. For example, Yazejian led a group of ELN colleagues to investigate the optimal age and duration of services for young children living in poverty to receive early care and education. The resulting paper, published in *Early Childhood Research Quarterly* in 2015, drew on data collected in ten cities (Chicago, Denver, Kansas City, Miami, Milwaukee, Oklahoma City, Omaha, Seattle, Tulsa, and Waterville, Maine) and based on approximately 5,000 young children who were demographically diverse. This sample and associated database that enabled analyses to provide emerging answers to an extremely relevant policy question—the timing and duration of services—would be next to impossible to generate without a network combining efforts to coordinate, develop, and sustain the work.

The network approach also provides a mechanism to design and implement other important and needed research—not only for Educare but for the broader field. For example, researchers and program leaders from four Educare sites collaborated with the NEP Team to design and implement a randomized controlled trial (RCT) of the Educare model. This study, which began in 2011, involved randomly assigning infants 18 months of age or younger to Educare or a control condition. The progress of these children has been followed through 2016 with efforts to secure funding to follow the children through Grade 3. Many label this RCT as the "modern" Abecedarian Study because it will compare the effects of a high-quality early care and education program on similar children growing up in poverty who did and did not receive the program. It also stands as an example of implementing a rigorous, "gold-standard" research method in a real-life program providing daily services to young children and their families. To spawn additional studies, the ELN has provided funding for Data Camps where the LEPs come together on a periodic basis with the NEPs to brainstorm open research questions in the current literature. Workgroups consisting of LEPs from various sites who elect to participate pose research questions and use the Educare Implementation Study database to conduct analyses to yield answers. Currently, numerous ELN Workgroups are investigating questions related to continuity of care in infant/toddler classrooms, peer effects, impacts of family risk and classroom quality on child outcomes, nature of services for young dual-language learners, and a range of other questions that will contribute answers to fill current gaps in the literature and to inform practice and policy.

It should be noted that the uniformity needed to build a cross-site network and resulting database similar to Educare's does not hamper local efforts to answer unique or place-specific questions. Each RPP is free to add measures based on local interest. Each RPP analyzes their own local data to answer questions related to their specific children, families, school, and community. Each site contributes their "core" or required data to the larger ELN pool and this aggregated data results in the large and growing cross-site database that, through secondary analyses, can be used to answer research questions with a larger and more diverse sample supporting greater generalizability of the results. Thus, the data from the Educare Implementation Study is used to inform local programming and services and to contribute to answering program- and policy-relevant questions of interest to state and federal decision makers.

While the Educare database offers many advantages to researchers interested in investigating program- and policy-relevant questions, its limitation is that it is comprised of children and families eligible for Educare. As an enhanced Head Start and Early Head Start program, to be eligible for Educare families must meet the Head Start and Early Head Start enrollment guideline of living at or below the federal poverty line. Thus, the large Educare database provides a platform for answering questions about children growing up in poverty.

A lab school research consortium could contribute to building a database comprised of information about children growing up in a range of economic and geographic contexts. Similar to the database produced by the Educare Implementation Study, a database composed of a comprehensive set of relevant measures administered across several strategically located lab schools, selected to offer both geographic and ethnic diversity, could provide researchers with a platform from which to answer a range of questions that we, as a field, have difficulty answering. An example includes the topic area of peer effects. Families enrolling their children in lab schools, like Educare schools, understand that research is part of the mission and are thus likely to provide consent to participate in studies as they are announced and implemented. This creates the unique situation where almost all the children in a classroom are assessed and thus allows researchers to investigate the impacts of peers on individual child development. Given the strong role many lab schools play in pre-service professional preparation, another void in the literature that could be addressed is to research features of various curriculum approaches with different types of pre-service students, enrolled in programs with lab schools, participating in a research consortium.

McBride and colleagues (2012) have written about and pursued federal and foundation funding for a lab school research consortium in the past. Reviewers, although positive about the overall concept and potential, voiced concerns about the infrastructure, coordination, and administration support required for a lab school research consortium to be successful. McBride's chapter in this volume provides detailed answers to many of these concerns based on his work at the University of Illinois. Our "lessons learned" through the cross-site Educare

Implementation Study and collaborative use of data among ELN colleagues also offer insights into the needed structures and processes for a lab school research consortium to be successful. This knowledge and experience combined with the current focus on early childhood education in the popular press, scientific literature, and policy arena suggests the timing might be right for funding the development of a lab school research consortium. Given that, what could such a consortium learn from the Educare work to date?

Lessons Learned: What Does It Take to Design and Implement a Multi-site Research Network?

My experiences gained as a result of actively participating in the Educare Implementation Study since 2007 and Educare RCT since 2011 have highlighted the importance of the following features in building and sustaining a cross-site research network:

- **Mutual respect and strong relationships among researchers, practitioners, and policymakers:** For research to meaningfully inform practice and policy, in essence to meet the promise of ADS, the voices of practitioners and policymakers must be present in all phases of the work—from framing questions to interpreting and disseminating results. Not only must these voices be present, a climate of mutual respect and trust must be established for optimal results. Applied to the university setting, researchers may be perceived as the higher status or more powerful individuals and this imbalance must be recognized and neutralized to allow the practitioners and policymakers to freely contribute their ideas and perspectives to ensure the resulting work has maximum impact and relevance. Based on experience, this is best achieved through the articulation of a compelling common goal—in the case of Educare the goal is delivering high-quality services to young children growing up in poverty to reduce or eliminate the achievement gap. While the researchers, program specialists, and policymakers bring different skills to the table, each is respected for contributing something valued to achieving the common goal.
- **Clear structures, roles, processes, and timelines:** The respective roles of the LEPs and NEPs in the Educare Implementation Study have been referenced above. For a cross-site network to be effective, leaders and followers are needed. The leader of a lab school research consortium could be an individual, or more likely a small committee, that would facilitate the establishment of basic policies and procedures with input from the consortium members. Participating members need to commit to common processes, such as a common core of assessments administered following standardized protocols on a common timeline, to allow the resulting data to be aggregated into a meaningful and robust data set. Lack of such commitment results in an incomplete

data set that significantly hampers and limits secondary analyses that can be so fruitful in producing policy-relevant answers.

- **Ongoing, multi-directional communication:** Despite attempts to plan and organize everything in advance, it is inevitable that questions and problems arise. The ELN has used regularly scheduled conference calls to discuss questions and brainstorm solutions to unanticipated problems or issues. Although in-person meetings have merit and are of great value in building and strengthening relationships, regularly scheduled calls are invaluable in addressing questions, keeping everyone on the same page, and keeping the momentum of research project activities going and on track.

- **Professional development:** The participants in the Educare Implementation Study entered their unique roles with solid qualifications. However, through participating in the Implementation Study, all staff have learned new things, especially new learning related to the conduct of Applied Developmental Science. Specifically, the researchers learned how to package and present feedback based on local data to partner classroom staff in more meaningful ways; program staff learned about the rigors of research and why standardization is necessary. The research network offered a variety of opportunities for professional development with some other examples including learning new measures, enhancing data literacy, as well as developing mastery with strategies for building the RPP, techniques for sharing results with people inside and outside the network, and processes for interpreting and using data to inform program decisions. As these lessons were learned, they were shared with newcomers to the network through network meetings, webinars, or conference calls and with the larger field through publications (for example see Guss et al., 2013 and Stein et al., 2013, for two articles published in a special issue of *Early Education and Development* devoted to the topic of the use of data).

- **Resources and infrastructure support:** As suggested by the above and elsewhere in this book, resources are required to support in-person meetings, regular phone calls, and other infrastructure required for cross-site collaboration. Thus, the identification of a funding source is critical to support cross-site collaboration. Based on experience, an important and often overlooked resource is time to collaborate. Lab schools are typically busy places with limited open time to add new responsibilities. This reality must be recognized and productive brainstorming is required to link ongoing duties to the cross-site research responsibilities. Drawing on the functioning of the Educare Workgroups, a motivation to collaborate is the desire to learn more about a specific topic and how the findings might inform local practice. For example, a group representing several Educare sites with large populations of dual language learners was formed to ask and answer questions about the impact of various amounts of home language/English used in classrooms on children's development of English and their home language. This group had high motivation to participate in the Workgroup because their schools' data was part of the analysis and the results held relevance for their classroom practice. The same would be true for lab school workgroups with the added incentive of disseminating the information to the college students who are the future of the field. While personal motivation is important, for sustainability this type of collaboration must be valued by the organization and incorporated as a component of personnel reviews, annual performance evaluations, and employee recognition programs.

- **Ability to speak to varied audiences:** Researchers often write for other researchers with the gold standard being the peer-reviewed journal article. While this builds the academic knowledge base, it often limits or slows dissemination of relevant information to those who need it or use it—practitioners and policymakers. Involvement of practitioners and policymakers on research teams not only contributes to asking meaningful research questions, it also results in dissemination of results to varied audiences through varied mechanisms. Typically, practitioners and policymakers rely on different dissemination techniques and venues than do researchers and this serves to get the information out to different audiences in a quicker timeframe. This enhances the impact of the collaborative work.

Next Steps

These lessons from Educare can inform the development of a lab school consortium and other research groups involving multiple sites and personnel striving to inform practice and policy. In addition to the above lessons, such a consortium would benefit from:

- **Strategic decisions about membership**—to represent valued and varied populations and audiences. Lab schools are often criticized for offering boutique-like services to homogeneous populations. To overcome this criticism and build databases based on a sample representative of the U.S., efforts must be focused on identifying, recruiting, and selecting lab schools offering services to varied populations.
- **A research agenda and an organizing theoretical framework**—to guide research teams to address existing gaps and to serve as a framework for interpreting results and building the knowledge base. For example, in addition to the logic model that graphically displays how the Educare model is predicted to accomplish its intended goal, the Educare Learning Network has articulated a research agenda that clearly outlines the scope of the research topics to be considered and the desired collaborators. Relative to the valued role of lab schools in professional development, Hyson, Horm, and Winton (2012) and Horm, Hyson, and Winton (2013) identify many gaps in the existing literature base on early childhood teacher professional development

in higher education settings that require investigation for our field to progress. A lab school research consortium could use the work of Hyson and colleagues to map or organize their collaborative research in the arena of professional development. The recent release of the Institute of Medicine, National Research Council's report *Transforming the workforce for children birth through age 8: A unifying foundation* (IOM and NRC, 2015) has confirmed the importance of a well-prepared workforce for early childhood programming to achieve its promise and highlights the need for more research to inform early childhood professional preparation. A lab school research consortium would be uniquely positioned to contribute needed research results in this area.

- **An identity.** In some ways, the saying "build it and they will come" applies. Given the increasing role of externally funded research on campuses today, many lab school directors feel the need to enhance their research activity and productivity (McBride et al., 2012) and a consortium may be a strategy for accomplishing these goals. Additionally, given the complex questions begging for answers in the literature, collaborative research appears to be the key for generating meaningful answers. Lab schools have different strengths and these can contribute to the building of a strong research network. For example, the NEP in the Educare network brings strength in advanced quantitative data analysis and this capacity strengthens manuscripts generated by the ELN workgroups.
- **A plan for growth.** Although it is wise to start small and design for early successes, the foundation of a lab school consortium should be built with an eye toward supporting future growth. All decisions must be made with a future orientation anticipating and paving the way for expansion, not to just serve short-term goals.
- **Funding.** As noted above, the idea of a lab school research consortium has been discussed for more than a decade. Many see the wisdom of the idea and are ready to join. The current context appears ripe for lab schools to join forces to develop a strong research consortium that would be uniquely positioned to address some meaningful and complex open questions in early childhood. A missing piece is funding. The authors of other chapters in this volume have also identified funding as a challenge. This gives rise to several questions, including: How can the group move forward without funding? What granting agency or private philanthropy is best positioned to support the formation of a lab school research consortium? What can the group do to demonstrate proof of concept to move forward and demonstrate viability for funding?

Although much work remains to build such a network, the anticipated dividends would be great. Such a network would offer:

- the power to address unanswered research questions in early childhood education, especially in areas where lab schools have traditionally excelled such as professional development;

- networking and professional development opportunities for lab school faculty, staff, and students to enhance their own research capacity and consequently that of the field;
- opportunities to cultivate and prepare future generations of early childhood researchers and to enhance the research profiles of lab schools;
- leverage for our field's ability to address practice- and policy-relevant questions. In essence to achieve the original vision of lab schools and to align with the goals of contemporary ADS, a consortium would
  - engage in meaningful and robust scientific research where "science drives application and application drives science" (Lerner et al., 2005);
  - conduct research that has direct implications for individuals in context;
  - design research that can be applied to lifespan developmental issues; and to
  - ensure research provides insights and implications for practice and policy.

The above four points relate to the definition of ADS and echo the original goals of laboratory schools. Additionally, given the increasing importance of externally funded research on university and college campuses, lab schools must position themselves to align with this research mission to remain viable and vital (McBride et al., 2012). A consortium of lab schools operating together to advance and promote meaningful research could be instrumental not only to the survival of lab schools, but also key to positioning them to thrive and achieve the original mission of lab schools that continues to be a high priority today and for the future—the generation and application of knowledge that is relevant to solving the challenges faced by young children and their families.

References

Educare Learning Network. (2015). What is Educare? Retrieved from http://www.educareschools.org/about/what-is-educare.php.

Guss, S., D. J. Norris, D. M. Horm, L. A. Monroe, and V. Wolfe (2013). "Lessons Learned About Data Utilization from Classroom Observations." *Early Education & Development* 24: 4–18. http://dx.doi.org/10.1080/10409289.2013.739543.

Harms, T., Clifford, R. M., & Cryer, D. (2005). *Early Childhood Environment Rating Scale* (Rev. ed.). New York: Teachers College Press.

Harms, T., Cryer, D., & Clifford, R. M. (2006). *Infant–Toddler Environment Rating Scale* (Rev. ed.). New York: Teachers College Press.

Horm, D. M., Hyson, M., & Winton, P. J. (2013). Research on early childhood teacher education: Evidence from three domains and recommendations for moving forward. *Journal of Early Childhood Teacher Education, 34*(1), 95–112.

Horm, D. M., & Warford, S. D. G. (2003). Bridging the gap through community collaboration: An evolving role for child development laboratory programs. In B. A. McBride & N. E. Barbour (Eds.), *Bridging the gap between theory, research, and practice: The role of child development laboratory programs in early childhood education*. New York: Elsevier.

Hyson, M., Horm, D., & Winton, P. (2012). Higher education for early childhood educators and outcomes for young children: Pathways toward greater effectiveness. In R. Pianta (Ed.), *The handbook of early childhood education*. New York: Guilford Press.

Institute of Medicine (IOM) and National Research Council (NRC) (2015). *Transforming the workforce for children birth through age 8: A unifying foundation*. Washington, DC: National Academies Press.

Lerner, R. M., Jacobs, F., & Wertlieb, D. (Eds.). (2003). *Handbook of Applied Developmental Science: Promoting positive child, adolescent, and family development through research, policies, and programs*. Thousand Oaks, CA: Sage Publications.

Lerner, R. M., Jacobs, F., & Wertlieb, D. (2005). *Applied Developmental Science: An advanced textbook*. Thousand Oaks, CA: Sage.

McBride, B. A., & Barbour, N. E. (2003). *Bridging the gap between theory, research, and practice: The role of child development laboratory programs in early childhood education*. New York: Elsevier.

McBride, B. A., Groves, M., Barbour, N., Horm, D., Stremmel, A., Lash, M., Bersani, C., Ratekin, C., Moran, J., Elicker, J., & Toussaint, S. (2012). Child Development Laboratory schools as generators of knowledge in early childhood education: New models and approaches. *Early Education and Development, 23*(2), 153–164.

Pianta, R. C., LaParo, K. M., & Hamre, B. K. (2008). *Classroom Assessment Scoring System (CLASS) Pre-K*. Baltimore, MD: Brookes.

Stein, A., Freel, K., Hanson, A. T., Pacchiano, D., & Eiland-Williford, B. (2013). The Educare Chicago Research-Program Partnership and Follow-up Study: Using data on program graduates to enhance quality improvement efforts. *Early Education and Development, 24*, 19–41.

Yazejian, N., & Bryant, D. M. (2012). *Educare implementation study findings—August 2012*. Chapel Hill: Frank Porter Graham Child Development Institute, UNC-CH. Retrieved from http://www.educareschools.org/about/pdfs/Demonstrating-Results.pdf

Yazejian, N., Bryant, D., Freel, K., Burchinal, M., & the Educare Learning Network (ELN) Investigative Team (2015). High-quality early education: Age of entry and time in care differences in student outcomes for English-only and dual language learners. *Early Childhood Research Quarterly, 32*, 23–39.

Yazejian, N., Bryant, D., & Kennel, P. (2013). Implementation and replication of the Educare model of early childhood education. In T. Halle, A. Metz, & I. Martinez-Beck (Eds.), *Applying implementation science in early childhood programs and dystems* (pp. 209–225). Baltimore, MD: Brookes.

8

WHAT CHILD DEVELOPMENT LABORATORIES NEED TO DO TO THRIVE

An Administrator's Perspective

Marjorie Kostelnik

At our University, the Child Development Lab (CDL) has a great reputation for offering a top-notch early education program for young children and their families. There is a long waiting list for children to enroll and the common wisdom around town is that as soon as expectant parents tell their families about the impending birth, their next call is to the lab school to reserve a future place in the program. This story is common across the country and I have heard it numerous times during my 35-year involvement in higher education administration and early childhood education. During this time, I have been a lead teacher in a lab school, a CDL director, the chair of a department that administered a CDL, and now I serve as dean of a college that is home to one. Based on these experiences, I have seen the value of lab schools firsthand, as well as their vulnerabilities. Most importantly, I have come to believe in their potential as valuable vehicles for 21st century scholarship.

CDLs have been contributing to higher education for over 100 years. Even so, no academic program can rest on its laurels and survive. This is as true for lab schools as it is for all academic endeavors. To appreciate the present-day and future roles of CDLs, it is best to start with their purpose.

Providing exemplary services to young children and their families is critical, but not sufficient for an early childhood program to function as a CDL. Founded on the bedrock of high quality early education practices, CDLs do more than teach children well. They represent the total academic enterprise: conducting research on child development and early education, preparing the next generation of early childhood professionals, and engaging with the community to improve people's lives (Elicker & Barbour, 2014; McBride & Barbour, 2003). Addressing this tri-part mission of research, teaching, and engagement has defined CDLs since the time of John Dewey. It is also what sets them apart from early childhood service programs on campus and in the community.

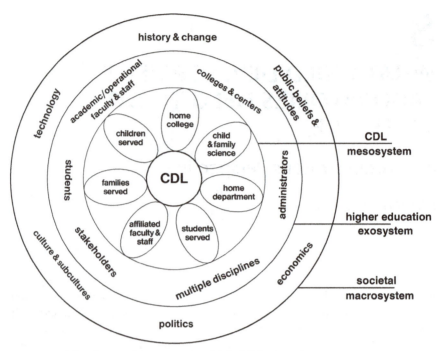

FIGURE 8.1 The Current Ecosystem in which CDLs Function.

To do their work well, CDLs must be in tune with the ecosystem in which they function. Of course that involves a complex mesosystem of their home colleges and departments; affiliated administrators, students, and faculty; as well as the children and families served. However, higher education is the overarching exosystem in which CDLs are embedded and to which they must respond effectively if they are to provide value to the institutions and professions they serve. In turn, higher education functions within a larger societal macrosystem that cannot be ignored. See Figure 8.1. With all these factors in mind, let's consider some current trends in higher education to better understand the dynamic context in which CDLs are operating.

Trends in Higher Education

The world of higher education is rapidly changing and the academy to which we welcome new students and faculty today is markedly different from that of even a few years ago. Public and private colleges and universities in the United States are facing intense scrutiny regarding their role in society, costs, and how well they are serving their constituents. The technology revolution, changing student demographics, and a growing emphasis on multi-disciplinary approaches to societal problems are all contributing to a shifting academic landscape. In fact, the early 21st century seems to be producing a "perfect storm" of external pressures and internal responses that are transforming higher education into something new (Altbach, 2007). Although many factors contribute to this situation, five trends stand out as game-changers for post-secondary education with significant implications for CDLs.

Trend 1: Public Beliefs about Higher Education are Changing

For more than 200 years, higher education in the United States was framed as society's primary means for enhancing the public-good (Marginson, 2014). People believed that by encouraging and subsidizing advanced learning the nation would foster the knowledge, creativity, vitality, leadership, and skills that could stimulate economic growth, technological innovation, and social advances (Mettler, 2014). That logic paved the way for increases in the number of two-year, four-year, and post-graduate institutions available to the populace as well as to defraying the costs of student attendance either wholly or partially through government funding.

By the mid-1970s the public-good perspective began giving way to treating college as a private-good instead (Hebel, 2014). This happened in conjunction with society's increased emphasis on the economic advantages of college degrees. The perception of higher education as a commodity whose primary benefit is to enhance one's pocketbook has increased as the correlation between education level and earnings has grown stronger. Numerous analyses show that advanced education leads to greater earning potential (Baum, Ma, & Payea, 2014). As the public has become more aware of this, they have become less willing to invest their tax dollars in higher education, believing that those who will eventually reap financial benefit should invest the most themselves. For instance, more than 90 percent of American adults surveyed said students who want a college education should have access to higher learning opportunities. Two-thirds also believe that students and their families should be responsible for the lion's share of the expenses (Mettler, 2014; Zusman, 2005). Thus, we are experiencing new realities in the nation's notion of why college is important and who should pay its costs.

In concert with this transition in values, publicly funded colleges and universities have experienced a steady 25-year decline in federal and state support (Chronicle of Higher Education, 2014). The latest U.S. expenditure figures (both state and federal) show that 36 percent of the funding for public higher education came from public monies, 48 percent came from households, and 16 percent came from other private sources (Baum et al., 2014). This makes the cost of a college education the second largest purchase most individuals/families will ever make. It explains the "consumer mentality" students and families are bringing to campus and why they increasingly assess the desirability of college majors in light of potential job prospects and the salaries students can expect to make upon graduation (Collis, 2013).

This trend has particular repercussions for CDLs. We cannot ignore that many majors associated with lab schools, such as childcare and early education, are low paying, especially at the undergraduate level. In fact, if one looks up "worst paying college majors" on any of several rating scales, special education, elementary education, child development, and early childhood education all make the list (Carnevale, Cheah, & Hanson, 2015). This makes it difficult to talk about the value of CDLs in the private-good terms that predominate today. Of course, continuing to advocate for better pay for all members of the early childhood workforce remains an important priority for countering this dilemma over the long-term. In the meantime, however, CDLs need to make clear their contributions to higher education overall in order to underscore the value they bring to their institutions. Strategies for doing this will be further explicated in the implications portion of this chapter.

Trend 2: A New Generation of Students is Driving Pedagogical Change

The U.S. Census Bureau recently announced that the 100-million strong Millennial-generation (encompassing individuals ages 18 to 34) is now the nation's largest cohort and constitutes the greatest percentage of students in college classes today (both on campus and at a distance) (Fry, 2015). Their presence is being felt in many ways, but no more profoundly than in the impact they are having on college teaching.

Obviously, not all Millennial-aged students are the same. In fact, this age group is extraordinarily diverse culturally, ethnically, politically, economically, and socially. However, they are the first generation to have been born and reach adulthood entirely within the digital age. Their lives have been immersed in the Internet, mobile technology, virtual learning environments, instant messaging, video games, and social media. They are used to having access to information on demand, to organizing that information for themselves, to creating virtual groups, and to sharing their thoughts, opinions and queries broadly (McGee, 2011). Brought up on Wikipedia, iGoogle, iPod playlists, and MyZone, Millennials have learning expectations that go far beyond a teacher standing in front of a room to lecture for 50 minutes, with students taking notes, and then leaving class to study alone. They are also way ahead of the idea that distance learning simply means reading text off a screen, contributing to a discussion board, and then answering some multiple choice questions. Their notions of what constitutes rewarding educational experiences are more personalized, more communal and more hands-on than have been the case for any generation so far (Cutler, 2014; University of Minnesota, 2015).

In recent surveys, young adults overwhelmingly characterized the ideal learning environment as follows (Pew Charitable Trusts, 2015; Teachthought, 2015):

- **Visibly Relevant**—Students can see a clear association between what is being taught and how it will help them in life and in their careers.
- **Engaging**—Students build on their prior knowledge and construct new understandings through probing conversations, reflections, real-world and virtual field trips, projects, and inquiry-based learning experiences.

- **Interactive**—Students and teachers co-create learning opportunities and experiences that emphasize playfulness, creativity, critical thinking, communication, problem-solving skills, collaboration, and teamwork.
- **Individualized**—Students have chances to select from among diverse modes of instruction and to make choices regarding content, the pace of instruction, and how their learning will be assessed.
- **Data Enhanced**—Students and teachers have access to data and data sources that contribute to easy modifications in learning strategies, teaching approaches, lessons, and curricula as needed.
- **Immediate**—Students access content and vehicles for learning 24/7. They receive quick responses to queries and continuous feedback from teachers and peers.
- **Technologically Flexible**—Students can connect anywhere, anytime, on any device.

To better meet students' needs, institutions of higher education are striving to create flexible learning environments that effectively incorporate all of these characteristics (Cutler, 2014; University of Minnesota, 2015). CDLs have much to contribute to this work. For example, they could:

- develop CDL-related coursework that incorporates multiple characteristics of the learner-centered instruction described here;
- model compatible learner-centered pedagogy in CDL-related classes (in-person and at a distance);
- formally explore the degree of effectiveness of learner-centered pedagogy through evaluation studies and research.

Such efforts are in keeping with all three facets of the CDL mission and have the potential to improve the professional development of the future early childhood workforce.

Trend 3: Niche Programs are Trending in Higher Education

There was a time when colleges and universities measured their worth by how many programs and degrees they offered—the more the better. In this way institutions built large collections of degrees, faculty, and facilities over the years (Van Der Werf, 2014a). However, an unintended outcome has been that many schools, regardless of size and funding source, now look very much alike programmatically. Although each provides choices to students, the curricula they offer are strikingly similar from one institution to the next. In fact, the level of duplication in higher education is of increasing concern to college presidents and policymakers, who point to the large number of such programs in each state and view them as unnecessary drains on resources (Van Der Werf, 2014b). This "sameness" is especially true at the undergraduate level, making it hard for students and families to differentiate institutions based on programmatic variables such as what makes early childhood program A different from early childhood program B. The subtle philosophical differences we academicians prize (e.g. a cognitive approach versus an ecological one) are often lost on consumers. And, although a few programs stand out, many do not. The result is a proliferation of programs that lack distinction and are losing their attraction to students.

To address these "generic program" dilemmas, institutions of higher education are becoming more interested in "branding" and in establishing unique programs that draw attention to their campuses. Although core curricula remain important, future projections indicate that the best opportunities for academic growth in student enrollments and research will take place within specialty programs or niche variations on the "norm" (Ermler, 2015).

True niches are hallmark programs recognizable to specific audiences: undergraduate applicants trying to sort through potential majors, graduate students looking for particular research and training experiences, new faculty seeking to build a career that is distinctive in its focus, and donors eager to support innovation. In other words, niches are programs people choose because they stand out from the rest. It is these kinds of initiatives that will likely attract new populations of students and faculty as well as external funding from granting agencies, benefactors, and policymakers (Lane, 2015). As an example, refer to Figure 8.2 to see how niche programs could be used to recruit students and to enhance students' professional experiences after they enroll in the program.

CDLs could play a valuable role in helping institutions establish relevant niches in early childhood. Although program specialization is not a new idea in our field, we haven't got it quite right yet. At times, we have had "pockets" of individuation within lab schools (e.g. programs that have adopted elements of the Reggio Emilia Approach or ones focused on infants). However, only a few of these efforts

---

- Recruit students to niche areas at both the undergraduate and graduate levels

- Intentionally build cadres of students with niche-related interests across disciplines and units

- Recruit a wide array of students to ensure diverse experiences, areas of interest, and cultural understandings related to a particular niche program

- Create opportunities for student teams to carry out 'real' work to promote their sense of efficacy within a niche area

- Promote team participation and collaborative opportunities in a niche program as crucial job skills

---

FIGURE 8.2 Using Niche Programs to Recruit Students.

have been leveraged widely across departments or campuses. Instead, lab school specializations have mostly "belonged" to the CDL, but not to an entire early childhood academic program, including faculty within and beyond the lab school. No matter how inspired such efforts may be, when they are disconnected from the teaching and research of faculty members not housed in the CDL, their scope and effectiveness are diminished. On the other hand, if a niche program were integrated both in the CDL and in the teaching and research programs in multiple parts of the university, visibility and the potential for academic impact increase. It is these conditions that CDLs need to cultivate.

Trend 4: Collaboration is Gaining Traction in Academe

A traditional view of higher education is that its members (both students and faculty) work independently of one another and that individual results are most prized. Certainly, the academy has a long tradition of supporting and rewarding solo accomplishments, first authorships, independent investigations, and teaching or conducting research on one's own (Lane, 2015). Today, that paradigm is shifting toward a stronger emphasis on collaborations to achieve complex academic goals. We are seeing more multi-unit faculty work groups and more transdisciplinary research centers. External partnerships with community organizations and businesses are also on the rise. Within the social sciences in particular, Applied Developmental Science (ADS) is gaining momentum as an approach to research, teaching, policy development, and community practice that addresses societal problems from a transdisciplinary and integrative perspective. Such a perspective provides a scholarly framework around which collaborative teams can coalesce and are doing so with increasing frequency (Burchinal, Howes, Pianta, Bryant, Early, Clifford, & Barbarin, 2008; Mashburn, Justice, McGinty, & Slocum, 2016). In concert with all this activity is growing evidence that successful academic collaborations can increase efficiency, improve instruction, produce stronger student learning results, and enhance scholarly productivity (Bennett, Gadlin, & Levine-Finley, 2010; Kezar & Lester, 2009).

In spite of these promising initiatives, higher education's track record in sustaining collaborative work is uneven. Colleges and universities are still generally structured around individual-effort models. Professional silos, hierarchical organization structures, and bureaucratic inertia get in the way of the more fluid work, joint obligations, and shared methods that collaborations require. Consequently, not every team is successful—some achieve only some of their goals; others fail altogether and dissolve (Bennett et al., 2010; Kezar & Lester, 2009). Based on mixed results like these, we know that genuine collaborations do not happen by mere proclamation or simply by putting people together in work groups. It takes more than proximity and good intentions to succeed.

The most successful collaborations are intentionally designed and strategically supported. At their core is commitment to interdependence, common goals, and mutual accountability. Without this commitment, groups tend to perform as individuals; with it, they become powerful vehicles of collective performance and impact (DuFour, 2015; Katzenbach & Smith, 2013). Variations in how people function can be portrayed along a continuum of interaction and integration. At one end is independent work, at the other, collaboration, involving joint goals and fully integrated methods, outcomes, and accountability. These variations are depicted in Figure 8.3.

The different forms of group work illustrated in Figure 8.3 highlight two things. First, there are different ways in which people may work together. No one formula suits every successful group effort. At one time or another cooperation, coordination, or collaboration may provide the best vehicle for achieving certain goals. Second, there seems to be a developmental sequence in how some groups progress from solo activities to forming true collaborations among individuals and organizations (Katzenbach & Smith, 2013; Lincoln Community Learning Centers, 2015).

For the past decade, CDLs have explored the idea of working together across institutions to increase their impacts, particularly in the research arena (Elicker & Barbour, 2014; McBride & Barbour, 2003). That work holds promise for the field and for CDLs themselves. Partnering among CDLs has the potential to increase the size and diversity of research samples, to increase CDL research visibility, and to appeal to the "teamwork" interests of today's Millennial faculty and students. It would also enhance the field's ability to address "big" ideas more coherently across institutions and regions of the country. Most importantly, investigating, demonstrating, and explicating how groups successfully navigate the collaboration continuum would address elements of "team" science that are of interest not only

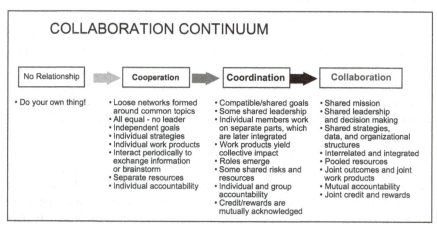

FIGURE 8.3 The Collaboration Continuum.

Source: Adapted from: Bennett et al., 2010; Katzenbach & Smith, 2013; Lincoln Community Learning Centers, 2015.

to early childhood, but to fields as far ranging as health and engineering (Bennett et al., 2010). Such work would be a significant contribution to the academy.

Trend 5: Higher Education Must Address Early Childhood More Coherently Across Professional Divides

Although the early childhood workforce is made up of many professions, academic preparation is siloed among several disciplines. Childcare providers, teachers, and health professionals are educated in disparate programs, departments, and colleges. Each profession has its own:

- History
- Philosophy
- Literature
- Heroes/heroines in the field
- Vocabulary
- Expectations
- Research traditions
- Paths to matriculation

Typically, students, teachers, and researchers do not interact across disciplinary or ecosystem boundaries, share experiences, or discuss best practices on how to work professionally with young children and families. Yet, once they get into the community, they may all be working with the same children and families, sometimes in concert, sometimes in isolation, and sometimes in direct opposition to one another's approaches and recommendations.

Responding to the lack of common training and pre-graduation contact among early childhood students, the Institute of Medicine and the National Research Council have called on colleges and universities to remedy the problem by becoming problem solvers and agents of change within their own institutions (IoM/NRC, 2015). Two tasks they identified are especially pertinent to CDLs. These are for higher education to:

1   build an interdisciplinary foundation of shared knowledge and competencies for the academic preparation of ALL early childhood professionals regardless of their home discipline (e.g. care and education, social services, or health/allied health); and
2   support consistent quality and coherence of professional learning across roles, groups, and settings for ALL early childhood practitioners in training.

The intent of these recommendations is to improve the consistency of the early childhood knowledge base, to enhance communication among professionals, and to promote joint learning opportunities for those being prepared for the early childhood workforce. In other words, it is calling for stronger ecosystemic approaches. CDLs are in a unique position to respond to these recommendations. They can provide a physical locale in which multi-disciplinary conversations and interactions can take place and they can offer common experiences, such as guided child observations, to mixed-disciplinary groups of pre-professionals in training. Such activities are compatible with the constructs of Applied Developmental Science, to which many CDL programs already subscribe and which are illustrated among the chapters in this volume.

Sample CDL Strategies Responsive to Higher Education Trends

The preceding trends offer insights as to how CDLs might enhance their effectiveness as well as potential challenges they must navigate in order to thrive (and survive). Taken altogether, they suggest that lab schools would benefit from expanding and diversifying their academic portfolios—broadening their teaching, going deeper into the research agenda, and developing stronger relationships across campus and with programs in the community. Clearly, CDLs cannot be isolated from the rest of higher education and thrive. They must be active participants in the academic community writ large. They also need to make the case that they can contribute meaningfully to the early childhood workforce as a whole (education, social services, allied health) and that they can help provide the means and the strategies to build a more coherent approach to educating the early childhood workforce across multiple disciplines in ways that are attuned to the current generation of students. With a healthy future as the goal, I would suggest that CDLs consider the following sample strategies. Readers will likely think of many more possibilities.

1. Expand Professional Development Opportunities for Students from the Multiplicity of Professions Serving Young Children

Professionally supervised, field-based learning experiences help practitioners-in-training translate the child development knowledge base into relevant field-related behaviors (IoM/NSF, 2015). Building on a century of experience of providing opportunities for formal child observations, demonstrations of best practice, guided skill development, and reflective supervision, CDLs could expand their work to support the learning of practitioners-in-training from a wider array of disciplines.

Expand content: Significant gaps exist in curricula associated with professional preparation in early childhood. For example, although the science of child development is a requisite body of knowledge in every field, not all professions have access to child observations and few programs offer in-depth work beyond the introductory level. In addition, only a small number include field experiences focused on bi-lingual children, infants, and toddlers, or meaningful interactions with diverse families (Bornfreund, 2011; Maxwell, Lim, & Early, 2006). How to use data in program development and evaluation are additional topics underrepresented at the undergraduate and graduate levels. These are all areas of professional preparation that CDLs could support more fully.

Include more graduate work: Currently, CDLs provide field experiences mostly for undergraduate students who are planning to be teachers in early childhood programs. This is important work, but fails to take into account child-related professional opportunities that require more advanced education. One of these is instructional coaching.

> *Instructional coaching* is garnering increased attention nationwide, in classrooms and in clinical settings as an effective means for advancing the professional development of practitioners (Aguilar, 2013; Jablon & Dombro, 2015). Enthusiasm for the practice is based on findings that practitioners involved in coaching tend to practice new strategies more frequently, use new skills more appropriately, exhibit longer-term retention of best practices, and do more to help other adults engage in best practices too (Marzano & Simms, 2013). CDLs, with their long history of training and master teachers, seem a natural setting for partnering with other faculty to educate coaches at the master's level. This would improve student prospects for higher paying jobs, provide much needed service to the field, and address the current generation's interest in obtaining advanced degrees.

> *Program leadership* is another area of need in terms of professional development and experiential learning (Kostelnik & Grady, 2009). Future administrators of childcare and community centers, school principals and superintendents, as well as allied health leaders need knowledge about early childhood as well as skills associated with how to operate child-oriented programs (e.g. staff selection, child assessment, and best practices for child programming). This content cannot all be stuffed into undergraduate programs. Master's degrees or graduate level certificates tailored to the specific learning needs of the various professions and carried out in conjunction with faculty from multiple disciplines are needed. These are content areas to which CDLs could contribute effectively (IoM/NSF, 2015).

2. Actively Support Developing Niche Programs in Early Childhood

Building a genuine niche requires CDL faculty and other faculty in a department or college to partner in developing the targeted program (e.g. working with children with hearing loss, nature education, technology infused learning experiences, etc.), in creating the curricula to support it, and in growing a related publication and research agenda. Ultimately, engaging with the community and policymakers needs to happen as well.

One does not simply "pull" a niche out of the air. The most effective ones represent unique foci that make sense for the institution, build on current faculty strengths, provide a vehicle for student recruiting, and offer a potential focus for new faculty hires. Niche programs address topics that eventually encompass teaching, research, and outreach and are guided by a strategic plan, including benchmarks and opportunities for formative evaluation. They are best supported through cooperative or collaborative strategies and joint outcomes. Finally, the most powerful niche programs utilize an active "branding" campaign to communicate key messages and help distinguish the program within and beyond the institution.

3. Play an Active Role in Facilitating Cross-disciplinary Interactions

At the heart of a recent Institute of Medicine/National Research Council (IoM/ NRC) report entitled: *Transforming the Workforce for Children Birth through Age 8,* is a recommendation that there be more cross-disciplinary interactions among the professions that make up the early childhood workforce. Clearly, the entire academic world needs to come together to do this effectively. CDLs cannot do the job alone. However, they could facilitate some of the conversations that must take place, provide experiential opportunities to students in fields beyond those traditionally served by CDLs today, and engage more actively with the whole range of child-related professions in the community. All of these actions are in keeping with the report's intentions.

Conversations

- CDLs could serve as hubs for workshops, study groups, and academic conversations for students and faculty across disciplines featuring co-leaders representing different professional orientations.
- CDL personnel could help form groups and/or insert themselves into collaborative teams that are forming on their campuses, relative to child development issues and topics.

Involvement in the Lab

- CDLs are ideal places to provide formal child observations or family engagement experiences to students in the many disciplines associated with the early childhood workforce (education, social services, allied health). Engagement in such experiences could be offered in person or through technology-assisted means and could be offered cooperatively or collaboratively between CDLs and other departments.

In order for this to happen, CDLs must do more than simply open their doors to others. Attracting students not typically found in the lab (e.g. elementary education, nursing, audiology, public health, or social work) will require customized interactive opportunities clearly targeted to their professional interests. This means going beyond simply fitting such students into coursework and practica originally designed for child development or early education majors. These new students may require more customized experiences designed around personalized time-tables, targeted methods of engaging with children and families, as well as pertinent assessments (best developed in partnership with faculty in relevant disciplines). Experiences for majors in audiology or medical school residents, for instance, may not be for an entire term/semester or involve the typical time blocks used by the students CDLs more often accommodate. Although such adaptations could upset long-held CDL routines, such joint coursework could enhance mutual understandings and create more informed communication among professions that have few opportunities to learn and work together prior to moving into the community.

Integrated Community Engagement

CDLs could partner with community-based field placements to provide extended interrelated practica for students. Early childhood students often have multiple practica integrated within their course of study, involving a mix of CDL and community placements. Such practica tend to be isolated from one another, with little or no communication between sites or intentional integration of knowledge and skills from one site to another. It is left to students to draw parallels and inferences and to reconcile differences in philosophy and approach on their own. More intentional partnerships between CDLs and community sites would be beneficial to students, who would gain more integrated experience, and for the sites themselves, leading to stronger channels of communication and professional support. Such relationships could be coordinated, cooperative, or collaborative.

4. Expand Their Involvement in Cooperative and Collaborative Research and Evaluation Efforts on Campus and in the Field

The entire field of early childhood (like all of higher education) is becoming more data driven. CDLs need to measure their effectiveness in terms of results rather than intentions and use data rather than anecdotes to tell their story convincingly (DuFour, 2015). Several chapters in this volume highlight how CDLs could identify, collect, and interpret data meaningfully on their own campuses and across institutions. CDLs also could work with community programs to support program-based data collection and interpretation of results as tools for program decision-making. In addition, CDLs can serve as places of inquiry and generators of new knowledge in child development and early education (McBride et al., 2012). The chapters in this book are all focused on strategies ranging from individual case studies to multi-site efforts that serve this purpose.

Most critically, if the call for developing a stronger research presence through the Applied Developmental Science-based consortium proposed by McBride in Chapter 2 of this volume is heeded, I believe that the field will be enhanced and CDLs will play a more central role in higher education. Such a consortium could include multi-disciplinary partners associated with individual CDLs and could position itself to address issues of coherence and convergence of the field's scientific knowledge base across disciplines and professional settings. Moreover, as a CDL consortium develops within an ADS framework, member institutions could pay particular attention to the work of "cooperating" and "collaborating." They could study cooperative and collaborative efforts, best practices associated with the collaboration continuum, linkages among partners, agreements, outcomes, pitfalls, and assessments. CDLs could also focus on the scaffolding needed to make multi-member networks more functional and effective. Such work would address the IoM/NRC recommendation for making connections across the field and contribute to our understanding of collaborations in the academy overall. I would suggest some additional ways in which this work and that of the consortium might be directed. Faculty involved in CDLs could:

- Use CDLs to answer accountability-oriented questions of interest to higher education stakeholders such as: What are children learning? What are students learning? What transferable skills follow children and students into settings beyond the CDL?
- Examine policies and practices that could provide models for any entity (in higher education or the community) to advance on the collaboration continuum;
- Specialize in cooperative and collaborative research methodologies, as well as strategies for navigating multi-site and multi-authored work;
- Specialize in developing and evaluating Millennial-friendly teaching and learning approaches within a range of disciplines encompassed within the early childhood workforce;
- Extend the work of the ADS consortium to include multi-site instruction (cooperatively or collaboratively) and the evaluation of this work.

Summary

Fueled by growing awareness of the importance of the early years, interest in early childhood is gaining momentum worldwide. Along with this is a corollary interest in those who work with young children professionally (IoM/NSF, 2015; UNESCO, 2008). Not since their beginnings have Child Development Laboratories had such a great opportunity to influence the field. The ADS Consortium model proposed in this volume is an especially good fit for addressing all the trends in higher education mentioned here. It gives CDLs a new way of talking about and demonstrating their value to students, their home institutions, and the field of early childhood generally. It reconnects CDLs to their original mission, more comprehensively and powerfully. It also provides a structure that takes advantage of this generation's strengths as students and practitioners, both in how they learn and how they wish to carry out their work. And, most importantly, it builds strength through cooperation and collaboration, both as a means for attaining outcomes and a subject for investigation. All of these conditions have the potential to address the challenge of providing a more seamless knowledge base for the early childhood workforce, which in turn will contribute to better, more effective ways to support children and families. Such foci are true to CDL roots and hold promise for a productive future.

Finally, referring back to Figure 8.1, I would propose a revision to the diagram and the current reality it represents. Presently, there are hard boundaries between most CDLs, the mesosystems in which they reside, and the larger milieux of higher education. The recommendations made within this chapter require CDLs to venture more boldly into the exosystem of higher education, both to influence that system and to respond more effectively to its dynamics. If this occurs, the boundaries between mesosystem and exosystem will become more permeable, enabling greater flow and collaboration among people, information, goals, and activities. See Figure 8.4. Ultimately, the current exosystem could become the new CDL mesosystem—enlarged, more complex, more multi-disciplinary, and more integrated. Such a state of affairs would benefit the system as a whole,

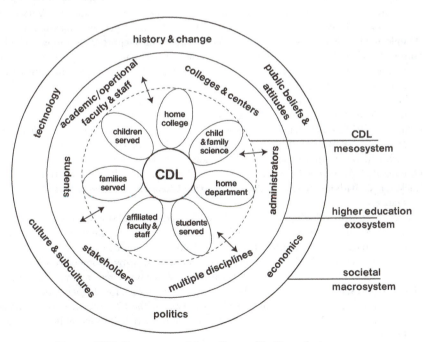

FIGURE 8.4 Future CDL Ecosystem—More Permeable Boundaries.

leading to increased relevance and powerful impacts for CDLs and for higher education, with better outcomes for children, families, and the professionals who work on their behalf.

References

Aguilar, E. (2013). *The art of coaching: Effective strategies for school transformation*. San Francisco, CA: Jossey Bass.

Altbach, P. G. (2007). *Global perspectives in higher education* (vol. 10). Rotterdam, Netherlands: Sense Publishers.

Baum, S., Ma, J., & Payea, K. (2014). *Education pays 2013*. College Board Benefits of Higher Education to individuals and society. https://trends.collegeboard.org/sites/default/files/education-pays-2013-full-report-022714.pdf.

Bennett, L. M., Gadlin, H., & Levine-Finley, S. (2010). *Collaboration and team science: A field guide*. Washington, DC: National Institutes of Health. Retrieved November 10, 2015, from https://ccrod.cancer.gov/confluence/download/attachments/47284665/TeamScience_FieldGuide.pdf?version=2&modificationDate=1285330231523

Bornfreund, L. A. (2011). *Getting in sync: Revamping licensing and preparation for teachers in pre-K, kindergarten and the early grades*. Washington, DC: New America Foundation.

Burchinal, M., Howes, C., Pianta, R., Bryant, D., Early, D., Clifford, R., & Barbarin, O. (2008). Predicting child outcomes at the end of kindergarten from the quality of pre-kindergarten teacher–child interactions and instruction. *Applied Developmental Science, 12*(3), 140–153.

Carnevale, A. P., Cheah, B., & Hanson, A. R. (2015). *The economic value of college majors*. Washington, DC: Georgetown University, Center on Education and the Workforce. Retrieved December 12, 2015, from https://cew.georgetown.edu/wp-content/uploads/The-Economic-Value-of-College-Majors-Full-Report-Web.compressed.pdf

Chronicle of Higher Education. (2014). 25 years of declining state support for public colleges. Data, March 3. Retrieved November 21, 2105, from http://chronicle.com/interactives/statesupport

Collis, J. (2013). The student as consumer. *Evolution 8–23*. Retrieved January 12, 2015, from http://evolution.com/opinions/student-as-consumer/

Cutler, Z. (2014). Unexpected ways millenials are impacting higher education. *Huffington Post Education*. Retrieved November 29, 2015, from http://www.huffingtonpost.com/zach-cutler/how-millennials-impacteducation_b_5604865.html

DuFour, R. (2015). *In praise of American educators*. Bloomington, IN: Solution Tree Press.

Elicker, J., & Barbour, N. (Eds.). (2014). *University laboratory schools*. New York: Taylor and Francis.

Ermler, K. (2015). Finding the niche in higher education. *SEEN Magazine*. http://www.seenmagazine.us/articles/article-detail/articleid/5053/finding-the-niche-in-highereducation.aspx, SouthEast Education Network, August 24.

Fry, R. (2015, January 16). This year, millenials will overtake baby boomers. Pew Research Center. Retrieved November 29, 2015, from http://www.pewresearch.org/author/rfry

Hebel, S. (2014, March 2). From public good to private good: How higher education got to a tipping point. *The Chronicle of Higher Education, The Chronicle Review*. Retrieved November 28, 2015, from http://chronicle.com/article/From-Public-Good-to-Private/145061

Institute of Medicine (IOM) and National Research Council (NRC) (2015). *Transforming the workforce for children birth through age 8: A unifying foundation.* Washington, DC: The National Academies Press.

Jablon, J., & Dombro, A. L. (2015). Effective coaching: What's your stance? *Young Children, 70*(5), 14–19.

Katzenbach, J. R., & Smith, D. K. (2013). *The discipline of teams* (pp. 35–53). Boston, MA: Harvard Business Review 10 Must Reads on Teams.

Kezar, A., & Lester, J. (2009). *Organizing higher education for collaboration.* San Francisco, CA: Jossey-Bass.

Kostelnik, M. J., & Grady, M. (2009). *Getting it right from the start: The principal's guide to early childhood education.* Thousand Oaks, CA: Corwin

Lane, J. (2015). *Higher education reconsidered: Executing change to drive collective impact.* Albany, NY: State University of New York Press.

Lincoln Community Learning Centers. (2015). *Collaboration continuum.* Lincoln, NE: Lincoln CLC.

Marginson, S. (2014). Higher education and public good: A global study. In G. Goastellec & F. Picard (Eds.), *Higher education in societies: A multi scale perspective* (pp. 51–71). Rotterdam: Sense Publishers.

Marzano, R. J., & Simms, J. A. (2013). *Coaching classroom instruction.* Bloomington, IN: Marzano Research.

Mashburn, A., Justice, L. M., McGinty, A., & Slocum, L. (2016). The impacts of scalable intervention on the language and literacy development of rural pre-kindergarteners. *Applied Developmental Science, 20*(1), 61–78.

Maxwell, K. L., Lim, C. I., & Early, D. M. (2006). *Early childhood teacher preparation programs in the United States: National report.* Chapel Hill, NC: University of North Carolina, Frank Porter Graham Child Development Institute.

McBride, B. A., & Barbour, N. E. (2003). *Bridging the gap between theory, research, and practice: The role of child development laboratory programs in early childhood education.* Oxford, UK: Elsevier JAI.

McBride, B. A., Groves, M., Barbour, N., Horm, D., Stremmel, A., Lash, M., Bersani, C., Ratekin, C., Moran, J., Elicker, J., & Toussaint, S. (2012). Child Development Laboratory schools as generators of knowledge in early childhood education: New models and approaches. *Early Education and Development, 23*(2), 153–164.

McGee, J. B. (2011). Teaching millennials. Pittsburgh, PA: University of Pittsburgh Laboratory for Educational Technology. Retrieved December 1, 2015, from http://www.ame.pitt.edu/documents/McGee_Millennials.pdf

Mettler, S. (2014). Equalizers no more: Politics thwart colleges' role in upward mobility. *The Chronicle of Higher Education. The Chronicle Review.* March 2. Retrieved November 28, 2015, from http://chronicle.com/article/Equalizers-No-More/144999

Pew Charitable Trusts. (2015). Pew's analysis of data from the U.S. Office of Management and Budget. *Historical Tables,* February 2015 and National Association of State Budget Officers, *State Expenditure Report,* November 2014.

Teachthought. (2015). *9 characteristics of 21st century learning.* Retrieved December 1, 2015, from http://www.teachthought.com/the-future-of-learning/9-characteristics-of-21st-century-learning

UNESCO. (2008). *The contribution of early childhood to a sustainable society.* Paris: UNESCO. Retrieved December 1, 2015, from http://www.oei.es/decada/unesco_infancia.pdf

University of Minnesota. (2015). *Student vs. instructor classroom.* Center for Educational Innovation. Retrieved November 22, 2015, from http://cei.umn.edu/support-services/tutorials/active-learning-lassrooms/student-vs-instructor-classroom.

Van der Werf, M. (2014a, January 10). Colleges are cracked mirror images of one another. *Future of Higher Education.* Retrieved December 10, 2015, from http://collegeof2020.com/colleges-are-cracked-mirrorimages-of-one-another.

Van Der Werf, M. (2014b, April 21). Universities are department stores—Is that a good thing? *Future of Higher Education.* Retrieved November 1, 2015, from http://collegeof2020.com/universities-are-department-stores-is-that-a-good-thing

Zusman, A. (2005). *American higher education in the twenty-first century: Social, political and economic challenges.* In P. G. Altbach, R. O. Berndahl, & P. J. Gumport (Eds.). (pp. 115–148). Baltimore: John Hopkins University Press.

INDEX